Contents

Acknowledgements

There are a number of people who contributed to this research. First, I would like to thank the Joseph Rowntree Foundation for their financial support for the study. Donald Hirsch, JRF programme adviser and Mark Hinman, JRF project manager both provided valuable advice and support. Members of the Advisory Group for this study also provided support and comments at each stage of the research, and their involvement has been especially helpful.

At the National Centre for Social Research, I am very grateful for the help received from a number of staff: Jane Ritchie and Dawn Snape assisted with the early development of the study; Margaret Blake provided key advice and support for the selection of respondents from the Family Resources Survey; Tim Harries helped to ensure the smooth running of the project; Marion Clayden and Jill Keegan carried out the in-depth interviews with great skill and sensitivity; and Alice Mowlam, Dan Philo and Mike Tibble provided valuable help with the data analysis.

Most importantly, I would like to thank all the people who very generously gave up their time to take part in the study and share their experiences and views.

Money, choice and control

The financial circumstances of early retirement

Sue Arthur

The POLICY PRESS

First published in Great Britain in December 2003 by

The Policy Press
Fourth Floor, Beacon House
Queen's Road
Bristol BS8 1QU
UK

Tel no +44 (0)117 331 4054
Fax no +44 (0)117 331 4093
E-mail tpp-info@bristol.ac.uk
www.policypress.org.uk

© National Centre for Social Research 2003

Published for the Joseph Rowntree Foundation by The Policy Press

ISBN 1 86134 476 7

Sue Arthur is a Research Director in the Qualitative Research Unit at the National Centre for Social Research. She is responsible for the conduct of qualitative studies in a range of social policy areas, and has a particular interest in research on family policy issues. She also teaches regularly on qualitative research methods courses.

The **Joseph Rowntree Foundation** has supported this project as part of its programme of research and innovative development projects, which it hopes will be of value to policy makers, practitioners and service users. The facts presented and views expressed in this report are, however, those of the author and not necessarily those of the Foundation.

The statements and opinions contained within this publication are solely those of the author and not of The University of Bristol or The Policy Press. The University of Bristol and The Policy Press disclaim responsibility for any injury to persons or property resulting from any material published in this publication.

The Policy Press works to counter discrimination on grounds of gender, race, disability, age and sexuality.

Cover design by Qube Design Associates, Bristol
Printed in Great Britain by Hobbs the Printers Ltd, Southampton

Introduction

Background

This research was carried out against the backdrop of a growing 'pensions crisis' in the UK. A changing demographic profile, brought about by rising life expectancy and lower fertility rates, has raised questions about how provision for old age should be financed. At the same time, falls in the value of the stock market have contributed to falling values of pension funds, with a number of impacts for people drawing their pensions now and in the future. These include, for example, reduced payouts on pensions and endowment policies, and changes to the structure of pension schemes, in particular the rapid closure to new members of a large number of final salary schemes (as reported in the *Financial Times*, 24/03/03). It is widely accepted that the rules and regulations around pensions are highly complex and difficult to understand, and this combines with uncertainty about projected pension figures to create public anxiety about pensions (Tanner, 2000; Pickering, 2002).

At the same time, there has been a movement towards a greater financial responsibility for the funding of pensions falling to the individual and away from the employer and the state. This has come about through the relative reduction in the value of the state pension, the move towards increased take-up of occupational and private pensions, and the trend away from final salary scheme pensions. However, access to a private (that is, occupational or personal) pension is far from universal. In 2001–02, 4 out of 10 male employees and half of female employees were not contributing to a pension scheme. Among existing rather than future pensioners, one fifth of pensioner couples and half of single pensioners had no private pension (Summerfield and Babb, 2003).

Research evidence suggests that, on the whole, people's knowledge and understanding of pensions is relatively limited, and that there is widespread uncertainty about how to go about financial planning for the future (Hedges, 1998; Mayhew, 2001). In addition, it has been argued that some people choose to focus on dealing with present and immediate financial concerns rather than thinking to the future (Rowlingson, 2000; FSA, 2002). Work history influences the ability to access pensions, for example through lower earnings or fewer years paying contributions, and this provides part of the explanation for women's lower access to pensions. Women may also have an expectation that they can rely on a husband's pension, but this may then not be realised (or not in full) as a result of divorce or widowhood (Evandrou and Glaser, 2003).

These issues have highlighted a policy concern about lifetime saving for retirement, and raised questions about whether people are saving enough, the extent to which a voluntary pensions regime is adequate to address a 'savings gap' and whether and how people should be encouraged to save more (Sandler Review, 2002; DWP/HM Treasury/Inland Revenue, 2002). At the same time, there has been ongoing discussion about the age of retirement, and the extent to which policy should be encouraging longer working lives, through work retention policies or measures such as raising the age at which the state pension can be drawn.

The financial implications of early retirement

Within this context, there has been a related trend over the last 20 years towards lower participation in the labour market among older men. Analysis of the Labour Force Survey shows a dramatic change from the late 1970s to the mid-1990s in the employment rates among men in their late fifties and early sixties: in 1979 around 80% of men in this age range were in employment; in 1997 this figure had dropped to under 60% (Campbell, 1999). At the same time, the age where male employment rates start falling seems to have reduced over the same period, from the mid to early fifties (Campbell, 1999). This change is largely attributable to an increase in the proportions of men who were economically inactive rather than any significant change in unemployment rates. There has been no similar trend among older women, although older women are still less likely than older men to be in paid work. Given the concerns discussed above about financing old age, this trend could potentially exacerbate poverty and reliance on state welfare, by reducing the amount of time people spend contributing to a pension or other savings scheme, and increasing the number of years where they have no income from earnings.

A number of research studies have been carried out with a view to shedding more light on the characteristics and circumstances of the group of people who are out of work in their fifties and early sixties. Between a half and two thirds of men out of work in this age group report being 'long-term sick or disabled' rather than 'retired' (Banks et al, 2002). Other research evidence shows that the two groups of older men (45+) most likely to be out of work are (i) men in the bottom quartile of the hourly wage distribution, and (ii) men in the top half of the wage distribution who have an occupational pension (Campbell, 1999). These studies suggest the existence of pull and push factors in the move to 'early retirement'.

Two recent studies have investigated the financial situations of people who retire earlier than state pension age (Bardasi and Jenkins, 2002; Meadows, 2002). Both studies found that people who had retired early had a higher income on average than people who retired at standard retirement age, which is consistent with the idea that for a significant group of people at least, they retire early because they can afford to do so. However, this is not the same across all occupations: where people have a low-skilled occupation, their likelihood of having a low

income in later life is increased if they leave work early (Bardasi and Jenkins, 2002).

The current evidence suggests that the explanation for moving out of work before standard retirement age varies for different people: this includes positive choices not to work, financial security not to need to work, and lack of opportunity to work due to health problems, disability, or lack of jobs (Barnes et al, 2002; Lissenburgh and Smeaton, 2003). Increasing levels of dissatisfaction among older workers over the last 10 years suggest that perhaps more people would choose to leave work in the right circumstances (*The Guardian*, 2002). Financial security and health are both seen as important for living a fulfilling life. However, one study looking at quality of life in old age found that health was more important than wealth in leading to a higher quality of life, and interestingly that when it came to retirement, the most important factor influencing quality of life was not when someone had retired but whether or not they had been able to exercise choice over when they retired (ESRC, 2003).

The government has responded to the issue of improving financial provision for old age through a raft of different measures, including the introduction of new more flexible pensions, and has enhanced the targeting of state welfare on lower income households, through the Minimum Income Guarantee, followed by the introduction of the Pension Credit in 2003. Other policies have been aimed at encouraging people to continue working or to return to work up to, and beyond, state pension age, and encouraging further pension saving through improved pension information and simplified tax frameworks (DWP/HM Treasury/Inland Revenue, 2002). The final chapter of this report will review government policy in the light of the research findings.

Research objectives and outline of methodology

The primary aims of the study were:

- to provide a contextual understanding of the role that financial circumstances and awareness played in influencing the decision to follow different retirement pathways, in interaction with non-financial factors;

- to examine the implications of an early move out of work for individual access to and levels of financial resources, in particular pensions;
- to explore the impact of moving out of work before state pension age on the way that households plan and manage household finances;
- to add to existing knowledge about the transition to retirement, and to point to implications for providing support to people during this transition.

Sample selection

The respondents for this study were selected from among people who had taken part in the Family Resources Survey (FRS) between April 2000 and March 2001. The sample was designed so that we could select people who had moved out of work during their fifties (or early sixties for men), and who were in different types of financial situation following their withdrawal from work. People were selected who were aged between 51 and 63 (for women) or 68 (for men), and who had worked during their lives but were not currently working (or training). People were included who had said they were looking for work. We specified that people's partners should also be within the same age range, but that they could be working, or have never worked.

The sample was then selected in a purposive way from among this group of potential respondents. A number of criteria were used to design a sample that reflected the key characteristics of the group, and the ways in which they varied from each other. The intention was to capture a wide range of diverse experience within the sample. The following shows the profile of the sample:

- 28 men and 28 women;
- 21 couples and 14 single people (including divorced, widowed and never married);
- a range of ages, between 48 and 62, at 'retirement', and a range of ages at interview;
- a spread across broad socioeconomic groups and occupations;
- varying lengths of time since retired, from around 12 months to over 10 years;

- a range of financial situations: different levels of income and capital, and different sources of income (pensions and benefits);
- different work histories (including some women with only a few years paid work);
- a wide range of geographical areas in England and Scotland: the research covered metropolitan and suburban areas in Scotland, the South East of England, Midlands, North West and Yorkshire, as well as towns and villages in the South East, South West, North West, and Yorkshire and Humberside.

Data collection

Between December 2001 and April 2002, in-depth interviews were carried out with members of 35 households purposively selected from the FRS. Twenty-one of these households were couples and 14 were single people. Where couples were interviewed, a separate interview was carried out with each partner, leading to a total sample size of 56 people: 28 men and 28 women. The reasons for carrying out interviews with both partners were to provide an opportunity to explore two different perspectives of the same situation, and to provide an understanding of the extent of joint decision making and financial behaviour among couples.

Interviews were carried out using a topic guide that shaped the areas of questioning, but also allowed for responsive and interactive interviewing in order to understand the issues from the respondent's point of view and in their own language. Interviews lasted between an hour and an hour-and-a-half and a payment of £15 was given to respondents. Interviews were tape-recorded and transcribed verbatim to allow detailed analysis, which was conducted using Framework, a content analysis technique developed by the National Centre for Social Research (NatCen).

Reporting results

This was a qualitative study. Qualitative research cannot be generalised on a statistical or numerical basis. Rather it is the map of the range of views or experiences that can be inferred to the wider population, along with the categories, concepts and explanations that arise from people's accounts. Where patterns or associations emerge from the data, there will be value in testing the strength of these through statistical enquiry.

Any names used in quotations have been changed to preserve confidentiality. Quotes have been attributed by giving respondent's sex, their past occupation, their age and their financial situation on leaving work.

Through the report, the term 'disability' is used to refer to the social context of ill-health or impairment. The term 'impairment' is used for the medical condition or loss of faculty (for example, blindness, deafness, inability to walk). Reference to 'private pensions' encompasses occupational and personal pensions if not specified separately.

Report outline

The next chapter provides an overview of the characteristics of the group of people who have moved out of paid work in their fifties, and describes the range of 'retirement pathways' they have followed. This chapter sets the context for the remainder of the report, in providing a greater insight into this particular group of people.

Chapter 3 explores in depth the decision to move out of paid work, and the range of factors that people take into consideration when leaving work. Chapter 4 addresses what happens after the move away from paid work, in particular what happens to people's financial situation, and how they manage their money. Chapter 5 looks behind the effects on people's financial situation to the underpinning views and attitudes that shape people's feelings about their financial situation, and their decisions about how to plan for the future. Finally, in Chapter 6, the main research results are highlighted, and some policy implications of these results are drawn out.

Retirement pathways

Introduction

This chapter presents a detailed description of the range of circumstances and characteristics of people leaving work in their fifties and early sixties. In particular, the chapter looks at the way that the amount of choice and control over leaving work varies between individuals, and explores in what way and why choice and control varies for people in different circumstances. In the next chapter, there is a more detailed description about the reasons behind leaving work.

The context of early moves out of work

People were deliberately selected to take part in this research, with a view to representing the widest possible range of different circumstances and situations among people moving out of work in their fifties and early sixties (see discussion of sampling and of definitions in Chapter 1). In this way, we hoped to understand more about the sorts of people who chose or found themselves to be 'early retired'.

When looking at transitions out of work for people over 50, there are two distinct points of transition to take into consideration: the move out of paid work, and the move into retirement. For some people, these two points may come at the same time, for others they will be separated by a period out of paid work, or a period of intermittent and part-time paid or voluntary work. The overall transition is therefore towards retirement, although the initial move out of work is not necessarily a 'retirement'.

Equally important in setting the context of people's moves out of work, is the nature of their prior employment pathway or work history. The idea of 'retirement' implies a move away from a main job or a sequence of jobs that have formed a coherent work history with a clear end. However, as is well known, people's engagement with the labour market can vary hugely, and their work histories can be characterised by many moves between jobs or long spells away from paid work, as a result of redundancies, disability or ill-health, or caring responsibilities among other things. In addition to people with more 'standard' work histories, this research study encompassed people who had:

- done very little paid work, due to spending large periods looking after children and home;
- worked in a number of different low-paid, casual or insecure jobs, often for short periods at a time and interrupted by periods out of work;
- had a 'two-tier' career, taking a second main job after redundancy, but at a lower level of pay and conditions (including moving into working for themselves).

In other words, there was far less of an obvious or identifiable point of moving out of work for people with these latter experiences, but rather a gradual drift away from any further engagement with the labour market.

One way of categorising people's circumstances on leaving work, and of displaying the range of diversity, is to present different retirement scenarios or pathways in terms of a framework made up of the key dimensions that shape people's experience. In the next sections, this is done on the basis of four key dimensions. These create a framework that takes into account (i) the nature of the circumstances of someone's move out of work combined with (ii) their attitude or approach towards moving out of work permanently. The four dimensions used for this purpose are:

- the trigger behind the move out of work;
- the person's readiness for moving out of work permanently;
- the level of control over the move towards retirement;
- the degree of finality of the move towards retirement.

The first three of these dimensions all represent different aspects of choice over the move. For example, the greatest level of choice would be for someone who initiated the move themselves, at a point when they were ready and had complete control over how and at what pace the process happened. The least choice would be someone who had the move forced on them at a point when they had no intention to leave work, and with no control over the circumstances of their subsequent withdrawal from the labour market. In between, there are a range of positions representing greater or lesser choice along these different dimensions.

The four dimensions or spectrums have been divided into two sets of two in Figures 2.1 and 2.2 to represent the move out of paid work (Figure 2.1) and the transition to retirement (Figure 2.2) – these moves can of course happen at one and the same time. People's positions can be arranged along each spectrum, falling into different positions within each 'quarter' of the grid as a way of representing how people can vary from each other.

The move out of paid work

In Figure 2.1, the move out of paid work is represented by two cross-cutting dimensions: whether the main trigger out of work was driven by the employee or by the employer (or some other external driver), and the extent to which people felt ready and were wanting to move permanently out of work.

In the top half of the figure are represented the people who initiated their move out of work themselves, and while many of these did so because they were ready to leave work permanently (group A), not all of them were in these same circumstances. People who left work in constrained circumstances, for example, because of their own health or in order to care for a sick or disabled partner or relative, did so in the hope that they might be able to work again and not with an intention of retiring from paid work (group B). Initiating a move out of work yourself is not, of course, necessarily an indication of full choice.

People in the bottom two quarters (C and D) are all people whose move out of paid work was initiated by their employer or by some other circumstance, rather than themselves. This includes people who were made redundant, who had their contracts stopped on grounds of impairment or ill-health, or who were given an offer of early retirement or voluntary redundancy. It also includes people who felt obliged to leave work under their doctor's instructions because of the risk to their health of continuing work, and people who left work as the result of what could be called a 'crisis' situation (examples of this situation included the onset of severe or terminal

Figure 2.1: The move out of paid work

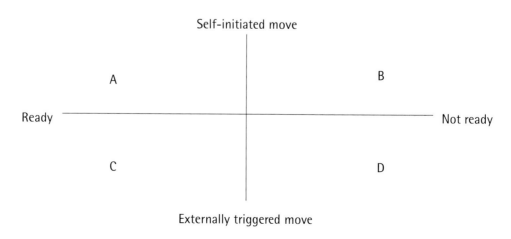

illness, or fleeing a local area to get away from a violent partner). There is a fine line here between people who took a choice to leave work due to constrained circumstances such as ill-health, and people who felt this move was forced upon them; this distinction may partly be a feature of the sort of language people use to explain their situation, or the extent to which people feel in control of their lives.

Where early retirement was offered or was seen as a standard option in their occupation then the move is initiated externally, but clearly in deciding to take up the offer people's position falls nearer to the centre of the vertical spectrum where there is also an element of choice. People who took up such an offer were clearly people who felt ready and happy to leave work (even if they had not previously considered it very much), and these people make up group C in Figure 2.1. Other people in group C fall closer to the end of the vertical spectrum where, although the decision to leave work was more or less taken for them, they nonetheless were ready and happy to leave work. Obviously, people who were not ready and did not want to leave work were people with little choice, whose move out of work was dictated by their employer, or perhaps to a lesser extent, by medical advice (group D). Where people's move out of work was driven by a 'crisis' situation, then the question of whether they were ready or wanting to leave work became an irrelevance in light of their dominant personal situation.

The transition to 'retirement'

Figure 2.2 represents the second key point on the transition, the move to retirement. Given the design of this study, some respondents had not fully completed the move to retirement, either because they were still hoping to find work or get back to work following time out through ill-health or caring, or because they were still doing some kind of paid work, albeit on a more reduced scale from their previous main job. Others had reached a retirement point, which happened in a number of different scenarios:

- at the same time as their move out of paid work;
- following a period of looking for or winding down work; or
- at the point when they reached state pension age.

The research study therefore captured people's experiences at different points in this transition.

The extent to which there was a clear 'early retirement point' was determined by a combination of people's feelings about wanting to work again and by their pension or benefits situation. For example, someone who wanted to work even if they knew it was unlikely because of ill-health did not see themselves as being retired until they reached state pension age. Some people had experienced a short period of time when they had been eligible for and claiming Jobseeker's Allowance after stopping work, but had been advised to claim Income Support when they turned 60, which they interpreted as being effectively 'early retired' by the state (this had sometimes caused resentment, and sometimes relief). People who had claimed a pension when they left work were more likely to think of their move as their final move out of paid work (although interestingly it was quite common for people to be reluctant to use the

Figure 2.2: The transition to retirement

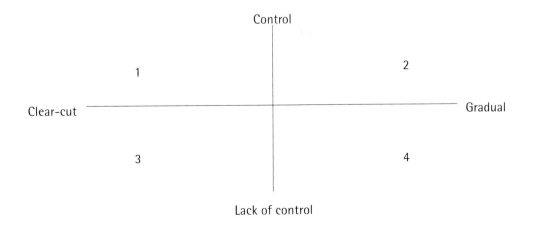

term 'retirement' even if they had no plans to do paid work again. This was because they had plans to continue to be active in a variety of ways, which might include voluntary work, but did not involve 'retiring' from society).

Figure 2.2 shows two cross-cutting dimensions: the extent to which the move out of paid work was clear-cut and final, or more of a gradual transition (as described above), and the degree of control the individual had over their circumstances once their paid work had ended. These do not represent a further four groups of people to those in Figure 2.1, but four sets of circumstances in relation to a different issue (that is, any one individual's circumstances would be represented both in Figures 2.1 and 2.2).

Where the move out of paid work and into retirement was clear-cut to a greater or lesser degree, people had very different levels of control over how this happened. One set of people had control over the circumstances of their leaving work, such that they chose the timing and accessed a financial package that they were comfortable with (group 1). Further along the spectrum, people had less control over issues such as timing or finance, but nonetheless were in control of the decision to retire. At the other end of the spectrum, people's circumstances more or less took control away from them, their shift to a position out of work was clear-cut but they had no say about it, for example because of the severity of their health situation or impairment (group 3).

A more gradual move into retirement can be characterised into two scenarios: (i) a controlled and deliberate wind-down of paid work, through continuing in a part-time or flexible capacity in an existing job, or through taking on freelance, ad hoc work (group 2), or (ii) a period of time spent looking for work after a job had finished but gradually abandoning hope of finding anything, because of attitudes of employers to older or disabled workers, and local jobs which were not matched to skill or ability levels (group 4). It was unusual for people to continue looking actively for work for more than around two years, although this was shaped in part by how near they were to state pension age, and their assessment of the likelihood of finding something appropriate.

Factors influencing different pathways

It is interesting to look at what appears to influence the level of choice and control people have over their retirement pathway. There seemed to be three dominant explanations for what shaped where people were likely to be positioned on the different spectrums or dimensions represented above[1].

The three factors tended to operate in interaction rather than independently from each other:

- work history and skills;
- financial situation;
- health and impairment status.

Each area is explored briefly in turn below (in no particular order of priority).

People's employment situation was central in determining their situation in a number of ways. Their occupation and seniority shaped their financial situation: their current and past income, and also their access to and ability to fund a private pension (the industry or sector they were in influenced the nature of occupational pension they had). It also shaped their ability to negotiate the timing and terms of their own leaving, including in situations of redundancies or ill-health/disability. Their skills and experience shaped the opportunities and level of control they might have over finding another job in their fifties, including making a more gradual transition towards retirement. Finally, their continuity or lack of continuity in paid work in the past fed directly into their pension situation at the point of an early withdrawal from work.

As is clear from the discussion above, someone's employment situation was directly linked to their financial situation. Where people had a comfortable financial situation and especially where they had the ability to access a private pension pre-state pension age (in particular an occupational pension), they were in a position to initiate their retirement if they wanted to do so,

---

[1] These are not of course the only factors influencing people's situation, and a qualitative study such as this can only point to apparent broad associations, rather than make clear correlations between someone's circumstances and the extent to which they are, or say they are, in control of their move out of work.

and control the circumstances of their withdrawal from work.

Ill-health or disability was the final key factor that shaped the type of retirement pathway someone followed. It was clear that ill-health and onset or deterioration of impairment affected the ability to stay in paid work, except in scenarios where they had employers who made accommodations to their job, but this was rare, and tended to happen among very senior employees or in public sector jobs (for example, if there was an opportunity to switch to an office job). The extent to which ill-health, impairment or disability had an influence was also shaped by how severe it was, and how much it proved a constraint in the light of the particular job the respondent had been doing (for example, one respondent had limited mobility in his arm and was unable to continue driving heavy goods vehicles).

Women in this study (as in the general population) were more likely than men to be in certain types of situation. If they had children, they were less likely to have had a continuous work history, and therefore to have had the opportunity to enhance their employment and financial situation as described above. The women who had experienced more of a 'career' pathway, had not always paid into a pension themselves. Where they were no longer living with a partner, they were often in a particularly difficult financial situation, with little in the way of their own financial resources. Where a husband had died, and his widow had the opportunity to have payments from his pension, her financial situation was sometimes better than it might have been if she had been divorced, but the additional strains of bereavement put a different set of feelings around wanting to leave work.

The influence of these three factors on the way couples and individuals made decisions about leaving work is discussed in far greater depth in Chapter 3.

Typical sets of circumstances

Despite there being a wide diversity of situations and ranges of positions, two broad groupings seem to emerge from the data. These are groups where circumstances tended to be associated with each other. However, they are not exclusive or comprehensive groupings of all respondents (as discussed below). They are not intended to provide an indication of prevalence of clustering within the population as a whole, rather a suggestion of association open to further investigation. The first grouping of circumstances describes pathways towards retirement that are shaped by relatively low levels of choice and control – this encompasses the circumstances in groups C and D in Figure 2.1, and groups 3 and 4 in Figure 2.2. The second grouping is of circumstances where choice and control are relatively high – groups A and B and groups 1 and 2.

Pathways shaped by lack of control and choice

One set of pathways tended to be dominated by relative lack of choice and control. People in these circumstances did not want to stop working, and even if they had initiated their withdrawal from work themselves, it was within a situation that they felt did not give them many options to continue working, or at least not in the way they wanted to. In general, this group were unhappy about not being able to do paid work, but had become resigned to this over a number of years. The two predominant reasons for moving out of paid work were forced redundancy and inability to continue in the defined job given a particular impairment or health condition. Being in a relatively low-paid job, and with either no private pension or only a very low one to claim on leaving work, was a consistent feature of such pathways.

There were different degrees to which people sought to find other work after they had left their job. Where people had been made redundant, the extent to which they looked for other jobs was shaped by their age, their physical ability, and their circumstances at home. Having a physical impairment, such as arthritis, made it hard for people to think of another job that they could do once they had lost their main job. At the same time, once past the age of 60 (these were all men), people felt that it would be difficult to find a job because of their age, or that it was too late to start on something new such as running a business. Receiving Income Support rather than Jobseeker's Allowance from the Benefits Agency created a sense that they were now seen by the state as retired, and should not be looking for work – this could come as a relief or as a rejection:

"And then I went to the dole office and the bloke upstairs said 'You're too old to get a job', he said 'You'll never get a job, not at that age…. So we'll put you on Income Support'…. I mean I never applied for anything … but I would have probably got a job." (male, was farm labourer, left work aged 62, received Income Support and redundancy lump sum of £3,000)

Benefit levels that were high relative to the potential income someone might earn also acted as a disincentive to look for work, as did the responsibility for caring for a partner at home.

For people who left work or lost their job because of a health problem or impairment, there was a similar set of issues when it came to thinking about work. Predominant health problems were physical mobility difficulties, especially back pain and immobility, and cardiovascular problems (heart attacks, angina). This was combined with being in a physically demanding job where they (or their employer) felt it was not possible for them to continue working (for example, care work or factory work). People found it difficult to think of ways in which they could have been helped to stay at work.

As with people who had been made redundant, there had originally been hope that they would return to a paid job, but after a couple of years this had been given up. This was less through difficulty in finding another job, but more because their health problem had continued or deteriorated. As time went by, people also felt that they had lost confidence in returning to a working environment, and had got too old to find another job or retrain. With this group, their employer and the medical profession both played a key role in influencing their feelings that they could not continue working. Where people were struggling to continue working, having someone make this decision for them came as a relief. Similarly, their interaction with the Benefits Agency could leave them feeling that they were not allowed or supposed to work or train if they were classified as 'unfit' for work:

"So that's when I got a note – a paper from the DHS saying, you are unable to work,

you don't need to send any more certificates in. That flabbergasted me. Because I've always worked. I wanted to work. It got me down did that…. That were like someone hitting me across the face with a cold fish…. I mean you can imagine getting that through the post. A hell of a shock. 'Cos I thought, I'll get better, I'll go back to work." (male, was a lorry driver, left work aged 53, received disability benefits)

The following case studies provide three illustrations of typical sets of circumstances within this group. The names have been changed.

Robert Gray is 62, divorced, and worked most of his life as a bus driver. He moved to an office job within the bus company after he had a heart attack, but was made redundant in 1990. He then spent four years working as a supervisor for a local authority until he was 54; he was 'paid off' by the local authority when he became ill with bladder problems, and his heart condition worsened as a result of an operation. His doctor told him if he did not retire he would precipitate his death. He sometimes regrets listening to the doctor, as he would have liked to carry on working. He received a lump sum of £9,000, and around £110 a week Incapacity Benefit and Disability Living Allowance, plus around £60 a week from his local authority occupational pension.

Kathy Talbot was working as a care assistant when her specialist told her that she should not work because of her arthritis; her employer had no other job to offer her. She was 48 at the time, and is now 53; she is divorced. She had worked all her life, in a range of jobs – hairdresser, factory worker, childminder. She was upset to leave her job as it had been her best and longest-held employment, but also felt it was too difficult to continue. When she stopped work, she received Incapacity Benefit and Disability Living Allowance of around £110 a week, and a local authority pension of £8 a week. She feels she is too ill (she now has angina and other problems) and also too unconfident to work again.

Mike Parker is 55 and stopped work three years ago when he was made redundant from his job as a trainer within the local council. He was given voluntary redundancy, but felt he had to take it because it might be his last opportunity to get a lump sum package. He had previously worked for the RAF, and then at a steelworks, before being made redundant in the early 1980s; he was then out of work for about 10 years. His wife has not worked since having children, and now has arthritis and is a wheelchair user. When he stopped work three years ago, Mike would have liked to carry on working, but he has now begun spending more time caring for his disabled wife, and feels it would be difficult to leave her. He received a lump sum when he left work of £10,000, and an annual pension of £1,250. He also receives Income Support and Carers' Allowance, and his wife receives Severe Disablement Allowance and Disability Living Allowance; their income from benefits is around £160 a week.

There was a final sub-set of people within this group, whose circumstances on leaving work meant that they could not really conceive of working at the point when they took part in the research. These involved crisis scenarios, placing huge emotional and physical strain on people, and where paid work became relatively insignificant, for example one man who had stopped work after he attempted suicide and was admitted as a psychiatric in-patient.

Pathways shaped by relative control and choice

The other main set of circumstances were characterised by a far higher level of choice and control. These tended to be people who were ready to leave work, although not necessarily permanently, and took up an opportunity to leave or initiated their withdrawal from work themselves. On the whole, they had control over the circumstances of their leaving work, sometimes choosing to wind down or phase out their work gradually, sometimes choosing to end in a clear-cut and final way. They tended to be people who were on relatively high incomes, and who were moving onto private pension incomes.

The following case studies illustrate some typical scenarios.

David Woodbridge is 60 and has never married. He decided to retire from his job as a computer programmer 18 months ago, when he was offered what he felt was a very good financial package, 'out of the blue'. He had worked all his life in professional jobs, including the civil service and the private sector. He had begun to lose interest in his job and was not totally happy with the conditions at work. When he retired he received a tax-free lump sum of a year's salary from his occupational pension, and a pension income of £9,000 a year. He has not done any work since.

Steven Marsden is 57 and left his mechanic job about two years ago. He had previously worked as a transport engineer, but had been made redundant twice during his career. He had always wanted to retire early, and decided to do so at the point when he felt he and his wife could manage financially; he was also starting to find his job too much effort, and wanted to spend more time with his wife. He has not worked since, and doesn't expect to. When he retired he had about £70,000 in his personal pension fund, which generated a pension income of £5,500 a year; they also received investment income of £7,000 a year. His wife had only done a few years of paid work during her life.

Paul Clayton took early medical retirement just over a year ago, when he was 55. He worked as a senior manager in the engineering sector, and had always felt he would like to retire early. He has a degenerative illness, which he had been managing at work, but his employer put the decision about when to leave in his hands, and he picked a time when his wife was also leaving work, and there were company reorganisations. He is now doing some voluntary work, but does not expect to do any more paid work. He received a medical retirement package of £200,000 pension lump sum, and £50,000 annual income. His wife, who had worked much of her life as a teacher, had not built up any pension in her own name.

Out-of-pattern circumstances

However, the two groupings described above do not account in an exclusive way for the experiences and circumstances of all people leaving work. There were examples of people who left work as a result of ill-health, and moved into a relatively low income situation, but who unlike other people whose paths were characterised by lack of choice, nonetheless felt happy to leave because they were ready to stop work. Mitigating circumstances, such as the fact that a couple could then spend time together, influenced their feelings about leaving work. At the same time, some people who on the whole had more choice or control over their pathway, nonetheless faced constrained circumstances, for example, where they chose the timing and circumstances of their leaving, but did so due to a deteriorating health condition, or a situation at work that they found too difficult to cope with.

There were a small number of people in the research study who moved out of work from a position of self-employment. These people had generally been working single-handedly, rather than employing others, in a particular trade or running a small business, for example as a mechanic. On the whole, their experience sits outside of the groupings described above: by definition they had greater choice and control over the fact and the timings of their leaving work; however, they also tended to have fewer options because they did not have the same level of security of pension situation as those in employment. The financial circumstances of people who had been self-employed will be covered further in Chapter 4.

Conclusions

It is clear from this chapter that the group of people who move out of work before state pension age is a very heterogeneous group: it is not possible to characterise their experiences as a simple set of circumstances. The main theme that emerges from this chapter is the way that circumstances vary in terms of the amount of choice and control people have. Choice and control applied not only to the circumstances of leaving one job, but also to the circumstances of being able to continue earning money, if desired, through an appropriate type of work before finally moving into retirement when ready.

People who seemed to have the most choice were people who initiated their move out of work themselves, at a point when they were ready to leave, and who were able to determine whether to stop work immediately or to make a gradual transition. People with the least choice had been forced to leave their job through redundancy or ill-health, and then had little control over trying to secure another job.

Having a choice about leaving work and control over the circumstances of retirement tended to be closely associated with having a strong financial and occupational position. This meant that even in situations where their move out of work was not something they had intended, people in a strong financial and occupational position were able to retain options in terms of the circumstances of their move towards retirement. Ill-health or impairment, in combination with the way that this was managed in the workplace, tended to place a constraint on someone's choices, either in terms of their own capacity to continue working or their wish to care for a partner. However, a stronger financial and occupational position allowed someone to control a situation of ill-health more easily than someone with lower financial resources and a weaker occupational position.

A lack of choice and control cannot only have negative financial consequences (as seen in Chapter 5), but also can have a significant psychological effect in terms of feelings of regret and displacement. Choice and control over retiring are important, but equally important in terms of financial effects are how and with what information decisions are made. This is the subject of the next chapter.

Making decisions about leaving work

Introduction

As described in the previous chapter, people moving out of paid work before state pension age had done so in a number of different scenarios: broadly speaking, through ill-health or disability, through being unable to find work after losing a previous job, and through taking an early retirement option. The degree of choice and decision making over this move varied considerably. This chapter will explore, first, the different ways in which people's decision making varied, and second, the range of things they took into consideration when deciding to leave paid work, in particular the role that financial factors played in their consideration.

Process of making the decision to leave work

There are a number of different dimensions that explain how people's decision making varied. These dimensions are significant in terms of understanding the extent to which people were in a position to make informed and considered choices, in particular in relation to financial considerations. They are explored in turn below:

- amount of time available to make decision;
- degree of consultation between a couple;
- level of awareness of financial situation;
- degree of consultation with financial advisers;
- degree of financial planning and preparation prior to decision.

Time available for decision

Obviously, the type of scenario around leaving work affected the amount of time people had within which to decide what to do. Redundancy was usually given with relatively short notice, sometimes a matter of hours, as were early retirement offers in some cases. Early retirement could be offered within a 'window' based on number of years' service, or with a short deadline within which to volunteer. It did not therefore necessarily come at the point that most suited the employee:

"... it wasn't something that I thought I wanted to do, take early retirement, but the job became so demanding, [and] it got to a stage where the law sort of changed with regard to education and I was 53, and I knew I'd got to work for another seven years if I didn't go straightaway because it was going to change and I wouldn't be allowed to go at 55, which is what I planned to do ... so I made that decision – it was a sudden decision." (female, was a teacher, left work aged 53, received pension lump sum plus income of £7,000 a year)

Where people moved out of work with an expectation that they would find another job, the amount of time it took for them to decide to withdraw from paid work altogether varied from just a few months, to around 2 years[2].

The nature of a health condition also determined how quickly a decision had to be made, for example a gradually deteriorating condition could be tolerated at work up to a point, whereas the sudden onset of illness or need for

---

[2] A Cabinet Office report suggested that most people had given up looking for work even earlier, by six months after leaving paid work (Cabinet Office, 2000).

emergency medical intervention required more or less immediate action.

The longest timescales were among people who initiated their own retirement, and people who were allowed an opportunity to make a delayed decision through a short-term contract with the same employer after their main contract ended. In these scenarios, the process of decision making could take place over a number of years, and in the case of long-term planners, could be said to go back many years (see below).

Consultation between a couple

It was rare in this study to come across any sense of disagreement between a couple over one or other of them leaving paid work. Decisions to take early retirement had often been part of a joint long-term plan, and couples often retired within a few years of each other, or at the same time (see below). Where decisions were made in a more reactive way to an offer from work, then couples appeared to have generally been in agreement about the way forward. Similarly, where one partner was having to retire because of ill-health or disability or being unable to find another job, the other partner said they supported their decision and agreed with their reasons. It did not appear that couples had always spoken in depth about their decision, but where they had not done so, it was because one party said they felt happy to leave it to the other to make the right decision. On the whole, people said they were happy if a partner was retiring as it usually meant that (i) they could spend more time together and (ii) their partner's health was less at risk.

There were occasional examples of situations where it seemed both partners were not exactly of the same mind: one scenario was where the husband was uncomfortable at the idea of his wife working if he was not working, especially if he felt it was not worth her working financially:

"She wanted to go cleaning, and I said 'Well you've got enough bloody cleaning here to do', you know 'What do you want to go out and...'. 'Yeah but' she said 'I get paid when I go there'. And I said 'Well it doesn't pay you to work. Your benefits you're entitled to you won't get'. If you do get benefits, if you earn X amount of money

you've lost them. And I said 'You might as well stay home and look at my pretty face'." (male, did a mix of casual work, left work aged 60, received disability benefits and small redundancy lump sum)

The second scenario was where a woman had been fully responsible for the domestic life and not involved in paid work, and felt that her husband's sudden decision to leave work would not only result in a loss of income, but would also encroach on her space at home:

"It came as a little bit of a shock I think. When I say 'shock' I realise that when someone retires that's another downhill isn't it?... [Interviewer: "What were you worried about?"] Well, I suppose I wouldn't do perhaps what I wanted to do, ... if I were to go down to hang some washing out I'd turn round and he would more or less be there, you know or something. But it's only because I've been used to being all on my own all day with my own company." (female, no paid work since having children)

Awareness of financial situation

Where people were retiring onto a private pension (that is, occupational or personal pension), they tended to say that they had a good, or even very precise, idea before leaving work of how much they would be going to receive from that pension. People had received pension projections from their employer or their pension scheme showing amounts for lump sum payments and ongoing pension income. Only one person, who had a number of personal pensions, said it had been hard to get figures for what he would get on retiring at age 55. Where investment income or a maturing policy was going to form a significant element of their finances, then people seem to have had a broad idea of amounts, but it is not clear that they were able to predict this with any great certainty. Similarly, where people were selling their business property as a way of realising capital on retirement, they often only had a broad idea of how their finances might work out:

"I thought, I haven't got a mortgage ... and I thought well you know with the pensions I'd have enough money and then with the capital I had left over [after selling business] I invested it in a bond which gave me another income. So I thought surely with all that I'll have enough. I'm not a big spender." (female, widowed, ran small business with husband, left work aged 59, £1,200 annual pension and £45,000 capital)

People found it harder to predict how much they might receive from a pension to be paid at a later stage, including from the state pension, or how much they might receive from a past, frozen pension. The focus when making a decision to retire was more on the immediate financial situation, with less of a precise view to the future (future planning is discussed further in Chapter 5). Only a small number of people said they had asked for a projected value for their state pension, in order to see how well off they would be, and there was at least one man who did not understand the projection when it came back. People moving onto benefits did not appear to have had a clear idea of what kind of financial situation they would be in. This is not surprising given the range of individual assessments carried out to determine eligibility and entitlement to state benefits.

In Chapter 4, we will look at the extent to which people's expectations did or did not work out as they had planned.

Consultation with financial advisers

Clearly, not everyone had the opportunity to consider their situation, especially people in constrained circumstances, who had to leave work rapidly. Even among people who did have a longer timeframe, seeking financial advice at the point when making a decision about leaving work was not common. Where people had spoken to a financial adviser, they tended to have been people taking an early retirement package, and who were in a professional occupation. Their financial advice had been arranged through work, either as part of a pre-retirement course or from an adviser who was made available for consultation. The advice was not described as having been a key factor influencing their decision to retire. Instead, people seemed to have been advised in two areas; first, how best to structure their retirement package to fit their needs (for example, trading off a reduced pension now for an enhanced

pension later), and second, taking the opportunity to buy extra years of pension through making Additional Voluntary Contributions (this tended to be among women who had not made full contributions during their working lives).

A small number of other respondents had been in touch with either independent or 'tied' financial advisers at earlier stages in their lives, when making general plans for savings and for retirement (see below). In only one of these cases was there any consultation with the adviser about deciding to retire: this was a woman whose husband's death had prompted her to rethink her finances and working arrangements generally.

Planning and preparation

The extent to which people had planned to retire early is clearly an indicator of how financially prepared they might be. However, people do not necessarily make good or sensible plans, and even where people did plan for early retirement, they did not necessarily have control over the exact timing of their withdrawal from work, which might come several years earlier than they had anticipated.

There were broadly speaking three different approaches towards retirement planning:

- no financial planning;
- broad financial planning for old age, sometimes combined with an assumption of retiring at standard retirement age;
- specific financial planning to retire early.

Where people had not really actively planned for their retirement at all, this tended to be because they felt they had never had sufficient money to build up savings or to put aside into a pension or other savings policy. People also said that they had just 'never thought about it':

"This pressure on people to have private pensions, it hasn't been in that long ... the only people that I know now that did have were people that worked like say police force or council, jobs that had pensions tied in with the job, you know. General workers, there wasn't a pension.... It's never really been a consideration. Not having money never ... quite honestly, it's never bothered me at all." (male, separated, was a taxi driver, left work aged 58, received Income Support)

There were also some people who were better off financially, and who had enough money to save, but who were relatively confident about their occupational pension scheme, and felt that it would provide them with the security they wanted without having to make any other arrangements. This was especially true for people whose job was structured to allow a full pension after, say, 30 years' service (for example, within the police force).

On the whole, married women had not planned for their retirement in their own right; where they did have a pension it was where they had an occupational pension scheme as an automatic part of their job. There was a tendency to assume that they would draw on the pension and other money accumulated through their husband's job and any joint savings. Even where there had been an opportunity for the women to pay into a pension fund, there was a general view among women and men that it was better to not waste the income on making contributions when the husband had an occupational pension himself. In retrospect, some women felt resentful that they had not been advised to plan more actively and pay their own pension contributions (especially in relation to the state pension). This was not described as stemming from a desire to have their 'own' money, but because they would then have had a higher level of joint money.

Broad-brush financial planning for old age was a more common approach than any planning with a specific age or specific amounts in mind. The only exception to this was of course with a mortgage, where people had often deliberately arranged for the mortgage to be paid off by or before the age when they thought they might retire (this included paying through a maturing endowment policy, as well as the completion of a repayment mortgage). General financial planning included building up savings, making investments, taking out savings or endowment policies, taking out private pensions or making Additional Voluntary Contributions. Often these general savings, aimed at having money for a 'rainy day', or to be comfortable in old age, were not set up with a view to be taken out at a specific point, and therefore had some flexibility

to them. They could be what helped people to survive financially if they ended up having to leave work earlier than they would have chosen.

"... towards the end we had some endowment policies which matured. Some of that we've had to, you know live on, some of it we've saved, managed to save.... So, you know looking back it's a good job we actually, you know saved money by paying endowments and pensions, been in a bit of a problem if we hadn't of done." (male, was a technical manager, left work aged 61, received redundancy and pension lump sums totalling £25,000 and pension income of £3,000 a year)

In some cases, financial planning had begun in middle age, for example people taking out a private pension in their mid to late forties. This was due to a combination of changing circumstances allowing more disposable income, and a growing awareness (sometimes prompted by advisers from insurance companies) that the state pension might fall short of expectations, particularly among women who were divorced or widowed and who had limited contributions histories. In some of these cases, people were making relatively small contributions to private pensions, for example £5-10 a week, and their contributions then stopped when they moved out of paid work less than 10 years later. Other women had been advised to make extra contributions into an existing pension in order to raise the level of the pension.

Specific early retirement planning tended to involve putting as much money as possible into savings, investments or pension contributions (in order to get the maximum pension), and paying off a mortgage at an earlier stage than originally planned if necessary. Here, as well, planning did not appear to revolve around specific amounts in mind, but rather maximising what could be done, with the resources available.

Influences on deciding to move out of work

The previous chapter outlined the main circumstances behind people's moves out of paid work. In summary, in terms of how the move was initiated, people could have a move forced on them by their employer, they could take up an offer of a retirement package, or they could choose to leave work themselves. When the move was a more gradual transition to retirement, there would also be a point when they chose to stop looking for work. The different financial implications in these different circumstances are explored below.

Before looking at financial considerations, however, it is important to recognise that there were a wide range of different influences for people in deciding to withdraw from work. These are represented in Figure 3.1 as 'positive' and 'negative' reasons, or could be thought of as 'pull' and 'push' reasons. They can be broadly grouped into personal, work-related and financial considerations.

Leaving work while still healthy, and hoping to enjoy time out of work before becoming too ill to do so, was a common theme and was often traded-off against being potentially worse-off financially. Many had a story to tell about a colleague or friend who had died before they managed to retire, or very shortly afterwards, and this made a deep impression:

"I've known a number of people, a couple of really sad cases of people who put off and put off and put off taking early retirement, and dying before they managed to do it, 'cos they felt they couldn't manage moneywise, and I'm fairly confident that you can manage moneywise if you flippin' well have to." (male, separated, was an unqualified accountant, left work aged 60, received redundancy and pension lump sum totalling £30,000 and annual pension income of £4,000)

On the whole, once people had chosen to make the final move away from work, they did not consider a return to work. However, people who had that choice forced on them had a number of reasons why in the end they felt they could not return to work:

- they felt they were too old to get paid work (a view sometimes brought about or confirmed by attitudes at the Benefits Agency or Job Centre, or by employer attitudes);
- they were unable to find another job that they felt was suitable for their abilities, and physical capacity;
- they felt that their impairment or health condition would make it very hard for them to work again.

As time went by, people began to lose confidence in themselves to be able to operate well in a work environment. At the same time, they valued the time they had at home with family or doing leisure activities.

Financial influences on deciding to move out of work

It was unusual for people to say that their financial situation was a significant motivation in making a decision to move away from paid work.

Figure 3.1: Reasons for moving away from paid work

Positive reasons	Negative reasons
Personal reasons - to spend time at home and with partner - to free up time for other activities - to care for partner, parent, disabled child, grandchild *Work-related reasons* - structure of job makes it easy to do *Financial reasons* - to take advantage of good financial package on offer - feeling financially secure and not needing to earn money	*Personal reasons* - onset or deterioration of impairment or ill-health - effect of bereavement *Work-related reasons* - stress of job or relationship with colleagues - lack of future progression in job - lack of confidence in finding another job *Financial reasons* - feeling it is not worth (returning to) working because it makes little difference to household finances

Instead, a combination of personal or work-related factors tended to dominate people's motivations. Financial factors were, however, very important in framing people's decisions about whether they should leave work or not: on the whole, people decided that they needed to or would like to leave work but then looked to see whether their financial circumstances made that a realistic option. As already discussed, some people were neither in the position to make a real choice about their work, nor did they have information about their likely financial situation if they were to stop paid work.

Financial incentives

Despite this, financial circumstances could be a key trigger or motivation in the decisions of people who were offered some sort of financial package to leave work: this could be for early retirement, medical retirement, or redundancy, and typically involved an enhanced lump sum or a gift of some 'extra years' of pension contributions. In these situations, people who had maybe not considered leaving work, or who had even positively not wanted to leave work at that stage, could have a difficult financial trade-off to make. They might feel pressure to take the money on offer now if they felt that what they might get on leaving work in the future would be worse, not better. A lump sum in particular was an incentive:

"… the way they worded it was if I didn't take it, they were going to keep me on for a couple of years, right, under a new contract and then they could get rid of me and I wouldn't get a penny…. So I took the £11,000 they offered me." (male, was a technical trainer, left work aged 52, received redundancy lump sum, pension of £1,200 a year, Income Support and Carers' Allowance)

"[I had been] looking to leave at age 55, which wouldn't have been the voluntary early retirement package and therefore all I would have had would have been a pension, it would have been at a reduced amount. But because they asked me to leave, the subtle difference is they make the pension up and of course give a redundancy payment as well." (male, was a bank director, left work aged 52, received

'substantial' pension lump sum, annual pension income of £35,000, as well as income from savings)

However, if people were keen to leave work anyway, for personal or work-related reasons, then the fact that they would be getting an enhanced pension formed part of their assessment of their circumstances but did not seem to be any more so than among people who left work without any kind of incentivised package.

There were some indications that people who had left work experienced a financial disincentive to return to work, if they perceived that the money they were likely to earn would not be very much higher than their package of state benefits.

The gender dynamics of financial consideration

Not surprisingly, financial factors formed a much greater part of the decision among people whose income was the whole or a substantial part of the household income. Where there was one clear 'breadwinner' (usually but not always the male partner), then for the partner, the decision to leave work was shaped predominantly by personal or work-related factors. The male breadwinner's move out of paid work dominated the couple's decisions about 'retirement', even where the female partner's earnings were not insubstantial. This may partly have been due to poor pension provision among women, and may also have been due to gendered perceptions of the importance of paid work generally, and of female versus male contributions to the household finances.

There were two exceptions to this general pattern. The first was among couples on relatively low incomes where the 'secondary' earner continued to work beyond the main earner, and at that stage their earnings therefore became a more significant component of their joint income. The second exception was couples where both partners were on similar salaries and with a continuous pathway of paid work, or career. Here, the typical pattern was for both partners to retire at roughly the same time, and to look at both incomes and both projected pensions in making their assessments.

Taking financial circumstances into account in decision making

It was typical for people to look at whether they could 'afford to retire'. This was of course especially true of the people who were choosing to retire, but even among those facing constrained choices, an assessment of their financial situation was part of weighing up the various considerations.

When looking at whether they could 'afford to retire', the following things were taken into consideration:

- an assessment of regular outgoings, taking into account that some outgoings would be reduced, for example, reduced or completed mortgage payments, children having left home, National Insurance Contributions, pension contributions, as well as changes in lifestyle;
- what a lump sum payment may enable them to do, for example pay off a mortgage, or invest with a view to drawing extra income;
- whether they had the expectation of future increased income, for example a way of boosting their income through earnings, or drawing a private pension in a few years' time.

Considerations of the amount of income that they would be able to live on were a key part of decision making. Obviously the actual amount seen as necessary varied from household to household, and was closely linked with the level of their earnings prior to leaving work. It also depended on whether they expected things to improve in the future when they were able to draw a state or (additional) private pension (see below). It was common for people to talk about spending some time (if they had it) prior to deciding to leave work, preparing schedules of income and expenditure and working out how much money they needed or wanted:

"... we did discuss it all, you know, and weighed up what he was getting, and what he were losing, and how better off we'd be, you know, and we decided that he wouldn't be – well, he would be at times, like sometimes when he were on call he got paid for call, there was all the extra money, but it doesn't matter, it didn't matter, you know – we'd got like the big things done – you know, the windows

done and all this new heating and that, we'd got these things done, you know, while he was working so we thought we could manage quite well." (female, was a lollipop lady, left work aged 52, had no retirement income of her own, husband retired with lump sum of £38,000 and annual income of £12,000)

As a general rule, people with a choice about retirement seemed to have felt that an income that would be roughly half what their earnings income had been, and a lump sum that was between one-and-a-half and two times their annual earnings would be a satisfactory amount to live on. One woman had worked two days a week towards the end of her career, almost as a trial period:

"And I had roughly worked out that two days per week would be roughly the sort of money I would possibly be getting if I took early retirement. In fact it was probably slightly more.... If I can manage on this money then I know if I do retire, then there's a reasonable chance if I don't get any paid employment I can survive." (female, single, was a lawyer, left work aged 52, received pension lump sum of £40,000 plus annual income of £12,000)

Sometimes the decision itself was made over a transition or trial period. Some people retired with a fairly secure knowledge that if they found they could not manage on their income, they would boost their income through part-time work; this was true of teachers who felt confident about getting supply teaching (but this is in some ways an unusual profession). Others planned to return to work, but in fact decided, when the return to work proved difficult, that they could manage on their reduced income. Others were not sure exactly how it would work out, but felt if their income became too stretched, they would just have to cut back:

"We thought that basically we would be quite well off, comfortable, hopefully, on one salary as opposed to the two salaries that were coming in.... I think we felt very much that it was an experiment to start with and it would take us a year or two to work out exactly how much we did need and whether the calculations had been right or not – and if they weren't, we would have to draw our horns in." (female, was a teacher, left work aged 53, received pension lump sum plus income of £7,000 a year)

Apart from when people planned for an 'interim period' (see below), it was unusual for people to talk about having looked beyond the immediate period following retirement in making precise assessments of their financial situation. In other words, in making their decision people appeared to focus very much on their income and expenditure in their existing situation, and did not look ahead to what their expenditure might be in the future in any precise way. Having some savings or investments were important to people, but more as a general safety net, rather than wanting to build up a specific amount of capital before feeling comfortable about retiring early. The only exception here was if someone had planned that a substantial part of their income in their retirement would be generated through drawing down income from investments; in this situation the actual amount of capital intended to generate income was more significant:

"I'd worked out how much interest I could get on a certain amount of money saved. I knew how much I could live on per year and what I wanted out of life. And I thought that I would be able to achieve it probably when I was about 55. I just went for it and that was it." (male, was a mechanic, left work aged 55, received pension lump sum of £70,000, and annual income from pension and savings of £12,000)

Role of financial factors when decision making is constrained

Where people were making decisions in more constrained circumstances, for example where they were being asked to accept redundancy or where they were feeling unable to cope with the demands of work because of illness or disability, then their decision was particularly difficult. In these situations, people had to balance up questions of their health and quality of life, and that of their partner, versus the knowledge that their financial situation was going to get worse:

"I don't think I was being very fair to John [husband], because many a day he wasn't well and really I was thinking, I should be at home, you see – so that was why, when it came, I knew we were going to be worse off, but I thought, well, it's better to have no money – and if anything was to happen to him, I couldn't say it, well, I should have finished at 60 – I suppose it's your conscience, isn't it." (female, was a shop assistant, left work aged 60, received state pension, and husband's disability benefits)

"We had a month more or less and we did talk about it ... yeah financially it hits you of course it does but there again what's the good of money if you've not got your health. You know I think it's no good being dead and having your money is it you know I'd rather he was alive and we had less sort of thing.... When there's two wages coming in and suddenly there's not it does make a big difference and you have to pull your horns in and decide 'well I've got to make do with what I've got'." (female, was an ambulance worker, left work aged 48, had no retirement income of her own, husband was still working)

Given constrained choices, the actual amounts of money that people were prepared to live on ranged greatly. They were shaped by the extent to which there were savings, whether there were debts, including a mortgage, to be paid, and other significant costs, for example whether rent would be paid by Housing Benefit, or whether there were dependant children who still required substantial expenditure, such as financing a university place. Another significant factor was how long people thought they would need to manage on a reduced income, and how they thought the situation would change once they reached an age where they could claim a higher income through their pension. At one extreme, one couple decided that the husband would stop looking for work, given increased pain and immobility in his leg and difficulty finding appropriate work. They did so having calculated that they could afford to survive for four years on an income from two private pensions of just £310 a month, by also drawing on their savings, including combined redundancy and pension lump sum payments of £24,000. When the husband turned 65, they expected their income from pensions to go up by another £700 a month.

As this suggests, one pattern among people withdrawing from work early through little choice of their own was to plan an interim period during which they would manage on finances that they saw as less than ideal, with a view to improving their financial situation when they reached a specific age, usually 65 for men, and would draw their state and/or private pension. Some people had a projection on this amount and knew roughly what to expect. Others had little idea, and were just hopeful that they would at least be better off than currently; nothing fixed was being planned on the basis of the money they were expecting. Part of the planning for this interim period was a recognition that after a small number of years, outgoings such as mortgage repayments, would disappear. Finances were sometimes deliberately structured to fit an interim period until state pension age in order to maximise entitlement to state benefits, for example by keeping pension income or savings to a low level in order to qualify for means-tested benefits.

Conclusions

When people were faced with a decision about leaving work, it was sometimes in very constrained circumstances. Some decision-making contexts clearly lend themselves to better or easier decision making; it is generally easier, for example, to make a considered decision, where there is a longer time to make it. Having a longer timeframe allowed people time to talk to family as well as become more informed about and possibly adjusting their financial situation, through talking direct to pension fund organisers and financial advisers. Financial advisers, however, tended not to have played a major role in influencing people's decision to leave work; where they had been involved their advice was generally in relation to how to manage retirement lump sums and incomes.

Situations of sudden redundancy or termination of contracts on ill-health or disability grounds allowed little opportunity for shaping a situation, and led to the most difficult situations, with reliance on ad hoc or temporary financial arrangements. Even with time to prepare, finding out about a likely pension situation after leaving work could be difficult and confusing, and finding out about benefits was even more so. Longer transitions towards retirement,

including staggered retirement between couples, and opportunities to continue working flexibly, allowed people more time to adjust psychologically as well as financially.

Decisions tended to be dominated by personal motivations, rather than financial. The stronger people's personal motivation (for 'positive' and 'negative' reasons) to withdraw from work, the less important their financial situation was, and the more they were, or had to be, prepared to manage on a reduced income. Given strong personal motivations to move out of work, people were sometimes comfortable about retiring onto perhaps surprisingly low incomes, although sometimes only in the knowledge or the hope that it would be a temporary situation. Where the personal motivation was low, for example following an offer of voluntary redundancy, then either a reduced income weighed more heavily with people or they required a good financial incentive, for example that they would be getting a full pension at an earlier age.

Decisions have to be made in the context of where people find themselves financially at the point they come to look at leaving work. People sometimes expressed regret at not doing more in the way of longer-term planning and preparation, and it was rare that planning was done with a specific view to retiring early. Despite this, people tended to feel that they were making the right decision given their current circumstances – balancing up the different personal, work and financial factors.

Where people felt that they had little choice about leaving their job, some expressed regret at not having tried harder to stay in that job or to find a different one; they were less happy with their 'decision' and where they currently found themselves. However, given the difficulty in finding an appropriate job, or an employer who was not prepared to take account of their impairment or health condition, they did not usually feel that there was very much they could have done differently. It was a relatively short amount of time, one to two years, within which people appeared to accept that they were unlikely to work again even when this was not what they had wanted. Perceived disincentives of the benefit system, and a valuing of health and leisure over work, also influenced people's feelings about looking for work.

Where there was an opportunity to take a balanced decision, people did weigh up financial factors alongside other considerations, and it was unusual for people to find themselves worse off than they had expected. However, their financial considerations revolved very much around comparisons of relative income and expenditure in the immediate or short term after retirement, including how a capital sum may affect their income or outgoings. This was done at the expense of considering future income or the role of future investments. We will return to the question of future planning in Chapter 5.

Financial transitions on leaving work

Introduction

Chapters 2 and 3 described the range of ways of moving out of paid work before retirement age: the reasons for leaving work, the process and the timescale can vary enormously. This chapter looks at financial circumstances after leaving work. However, the current study can only go part of the way to exploring financial outcomes or effects of early retirement. This is for a number of reasons. First, the research interview with respondents was carried out at varying times after the move away from work and at different stages in each individual's path. The financial effects therefore cannot be seen as final effects or outcomes; people's future situations are not necessarily firmly fixed within a few years after leaving work. Second, people found it hard to determine for the purposes of the interview how their situation might have been different if they had stayed in work longer, partly because of insufficient knowledge about their pension situation, and partly because they felt there were too many other unknown variables. It is therefore not straightforward to make an assessment of the specific effect of early retirement on their financial situation.

The nature of financial transitions

Following withdrawal from work, the financial situation could take some time to become established. This was partly due to initial difficulties in accessing benefit or pension entitlements, but was also due to changes in someone's work, job seeking or impairment status (all of which could affect their financial and benefits situation). In addition, access to finances and financial situation could change after the point of withdrawing from work: this could include acquiring sums of money (through inheritance or through a policy maturing), or starting to draw an income (from a pension or annuity, or from capital).

The extent to which people's financial situation changed after they left work depended in part on the circumstances in which they left work. So, for example, people retiring onto an early retirement package and drawing their pension immediately had a fairly straightforward financial transition from one scenario to another (although their finances may subsequently have changed in an unanticipated way). Where people's withdrawal from work was not chosen or was more gradual, then they also had a more gradual financial transition, with income coming from different sources, including changing (usually increasing) entitlement to a range of benefits. A gradual financial transition could be valuable if it enabled people to adjust slowly to a reduced income, for example where two partners staggered their retirement, but in other circumstances gave a degree of unpredictability about their situation.

Financial circumstances post-retirement are therefore determined by the pre-existing financial and personal situation, but are also shaped by the actions and decisions that people make on withdrawing from work, for example decisions on how to draw a pension (amount to take as a lump sum, or when to draw it), or decisions about how to manage their finances. This chapter looks at financial transitions in the light of these various contextual factors.

Financial circumstances after leaving work

People's financial situations on withdrawing from paid work appear to be predominantly shaped by their prior financial circumstances, in particular their work history and past earnings, during their earlier working life. It is therefore helpful to divide households into four groups according to approximate earnings levels, in order to explore the effects of behaviour and other circumstances, as well as earnings[3]. It is not the intention of this qualitative study to suggest that there is a statistical correlation between each income group and the experiences of people in this group, or that these experiences are comprehensive or exclusive to these groups. However, the presentation of data in this way provides an opportunity to suggest possible similarities according to financial situation, as well as possible differences linked to different circumstances or behaviours.

The income divisions used are necessarily fairly crude, given that people's earnings had fluctuated during their lifetime:

- annual incomes generally below £11,000 during their work history; from earnings and from periods on benefits;
- annual incomes of approximately £11,000 to £20,000;
- annual incomes of approximately £20,000 to £30,000;
- annual incomes of over £30,000.

By looking at households rather than individuals, it obscures the independent resources of married people. However, married couples in this study predominantly shared resources (and usually decision making), so there is a clear rationale for looking at them in this way.

---

[3] The government's Green Paper, *Simplicity, security and choice* (DWP/HM Treasury/Inland Revenue, 2002), makes a distinction between people earning below and above around £11,000 a year, in terms of whether they would need to make their own private pension provision in order to achieve a replacement rate of between half and two thirds of earnings. This was the rationale behind selecting £11,000 as a cut-off point between groups of respondents.

Households with low earnings

This group with low earnings includes people who worked in casual jobs, or a number of different manual jobs, and who may have had periods out of work. People in this group did not own their own homes. Although some people in this group had an occupational pension, these generally appeared to be fairly low; one was already being drawn, generating just £30 a month income for the respondent, and the others were waiting to draw them at 65, but were expecting them to be low because of having stopped paying contributions in their mid-fifties. In fact, one respondent was worried he might be worse off at 65 if he was no longer entitled to any means-tested benefits once he drew his pension.

All had moved out of work following redundancy or ill-health, or a combination of both. All were receiving means-tested benefits (Income Support and/or Housing Benefit), and most were receiving disability benefits, ranging from around £55 to £115 a week, depending on the eligibility and benefit level. On the whole, they were on a broadly equivalent income level to their income through earnings, especially once Housing Benefit and Council Tax Benefit were taken into account. People had very little idea of how things might change in the future, but were not expecting their situation to get any better.

Households with low to middling earnings

This group of people had a household income during their working life of more than £11,000 a year, but which had usually been less than £20,000. Among married couples, the woman had often never done any paid work, or done only a very small amount or at a very part-time level (for example, earning £40 a week). All had some kind of private pension, although not all were drawing this immediately on withdrawing from paid work. As with the previous group, reasons for leaving work tended to be redundancy and/or ill-health, and some were therefore eligible for disability benefits. Two men in this group left for reasons of choice, and had planned their finances carefully (see below).

Making financial preparation in middle age (that is, in their forties) was a feature of some people in this group, prompted by financial advisers from banks, or by a general awareness that it might be necessary to save more in order not to be in poverty. However, if people then retired in their mid-fifties (as opposed to 60 or over), they were disappointed to find that the private pension they had paid into was, or was likely to be, worth very little (for example, £200 per annum), because they had stopped making contributions earlier than planned:

"I paid a private pension. Only through Maggie Thatcher telling me 'You must pay a private pension and you'll benefit from this and that' and I thought 'Well if I don't get a pension for who I am at least I'll get what I've paid in'. And that'll be something that I've actually paid into. But that went down the drain in '95 because once you've packed in work you couldn't pay any more of that pension." (female, divorced, was a nurse, left work aged 55, received disability benefits)

People who were under 60 when they left work had chosen or were obliged to defer drawing part or all of their pension until 60 or 65. Where they had chosen to do so, this was in the hope that it would continue to grow and they would benefit financially from waiting. This meant that several people were having to survive a temporary period, where they were hoping things would improve, but were actually unsure about how much pension they would get in the future. During this period, people in this group were drawing benefits, sometimes at a low level. Because wives in the household were generally ineligible for any benefits, except for disability benefits, in their own right, this meant that the couple were surviving on one source of income.

Among those who had a reasonably clear idea of what to expect from their pension, or who had reached an age where they were drawing their final pension, the amounts of private pension income among this group varied but were often very low, for example less than £2,000 a year. People who had marginally better incomes from their pension, around £4,000-5,000 a year, had been in relatively stable and continuous employment in a skilled or semi-skilled job.

Not surprisingly, people in this group tended to feel that they were badly off, especially if they were still paying rent or making mortgage repayments; they had not anticipated they would be out of work so early and were unable to pay off their mortgage. The drop between their work earnings and their income on leaving work was significant. One or two people in this group also had significant levels of debt, and this caused considerable difficulty when they lost their income from earnings. They were looking forward to a time when they could draw a pension, although they were perhaps overestimating the amount of difference this might make financially.

Two people within this group stand out as having adopted quite a different pathway. Both were men with wives who had not worked, and who worked themselves in skilled jobs, but who had experienced at least two redundancies in their work history. Partly as a result of these redundancy pay-offs, and partly because of a desire to retire early, these men had managed to save well over £100,000 by their fifties, and when they reached a point that they no longer wanted to work, they just left. Neither had very substantial income from their private pension (around £5,000-6,000), but they drew on their savings and on the interest from their savings to generate enough income to feel that they were living comfortably (one man also had a disabled son whose benefits added to the household income). For these two households, their financial situation after leaving work was far closer to their work-based earnings than among others in this group.

Households with middling to high earnings

This group includes people whose household income from earnings was between around £20,000 and £30,000 a year. The husbands in married couples had generally had just one continuous 'white collar' job throughout their working career. They had thus had the opportunity to build up an occupational pension, which generated an income of around £8,000 or more a year. Their wives tended to have been in more semi-skilled jobs, working part time, or with a very limited work history. One woman who was widowed had run a small business alongside her husband; she decided to shut the business down when she felt it had become too much work. The men tended to have left work through choice following an opportunity to take early retirement, although one man had been made redundant. Health issues were also sometimes in the background of their decision making.

As well as having paid into private pensions, this group also had some savings (of between £15,000 and £60,000) and some had already paid off their mortgage by the time they retired. Others used their pension lump sum to pay off most of the mortgage, or expected an endowment policy to pay off their mortgage. When they retired, they drew their private pensions straight away, but because these were not always very large, they expected things to change for the better in the future when each partner reached state pension age and received a state pension. As with the previous group, it could sometimes be the fact that people had made good retirement planning through saving and long-term policies (even if not aimed at early retirement) that enabled them to manage when they retired:

> "... towards the end [that is, before we drew state pension] we had some endowment policies, which matured. Some of that we've had to, you know live on, some of it we've saved, managed to save.... So, you know looking back it's a good job we actually, you know saved money by paying endowments and pensions, been in a bit of a problem if we hadn't of done." (male, was a technical manager, left work aged 61, received redundancy and pension lump sums totalling £25,000 and pension income of £3,000 a year)

Although this group had made a decision to retire from work, it was often under somewhat constrained circumstances, and not with the financial situation that they might have ideally chosen. As a result, they tended to be somewhat anxious about their situation, feeling that they had to watch their money quite carefully, and looking forward, for example, to the time when the mortgage would be paid off. Among this group, there was concern about whether their pension would keep pace with inflation. Where pension payments were relatively low, disability benefits helped to boost their household income, but this led to some concern that their income might go down at the point when they drew their state pension. Using savings had also helped as an interim measure, but was not seen as a permanent financial solution.

Households with high earnings

This group is made up of households with income from earnings during their life of over £30,000 a year. Husbands tended to have been in well-paid professional jobs – accountants, senior managers, engineers. There were also a number of women in this group who had worked most of their lives, and made a significant or equal contribution to the joint finances. Households tended to have relatively large amounts of savings or investments (£50,000 and over) and mortgages that were paid off either before or on retirement, leading to high equity value in their house. A few still had a small mortgage remaining, but did not see this as a financial burden because of their relatively high income.

In all but two cases, people in this group had chosen to leave work when they did, although a couple of respondents in this group also made their decision in the light of deteriorating health. Apart from the two men who were made redundant, all had claimed their pension immediately on retiring: pension income ranged from around £12,000 to £40,000 a year (the variation being shaped primarily by salary prior to retirement). The other two were waiting until they reached standard retirement age in order to maximise their pension payments, which they recognised were lower because they had stopped making contributions. In one case, the couple were living off what were substantial savings, and in the other, the wife had drawn her teacher's pension as income, and had in fact then gone back to work part time to supplement their income.

On the whole, this group were happy with their situation, and felt that they were comfortably off. People who had a household income of roughly half their working income appeared to feel that this was a comfortable amount to live off. As with the previous group, people at the lower end of the income range expressed some anxiety about their finances, with concern about ensuring money was invested well, and a sense of vulnerability about relying on investments. On the whole, people did not expect their situation to change greatly at the point when they claimed their state pension.

Self-employment

People who had been self-employed formed only a very small part of the research sample. However, their circumstances were sufficiently different from employed people to merit a separate description.

Circumstances of leaving self-employment are inevitably somewhat different to leaving an employed job. Depending on the nature of the work, there is likely to be more control over the time and circumstances, for example if it involves selling up a business property, or turning down any new work opportunities; in this study, personal reasons rather than financial or work-related reasons, dominated the decisions of self-employed people to stop working. People who have been self-employed are less likely to have had the opportunity to build up a personal pension, or to have paid National Insurance Contributions, and this tended to be the case among these respondents. Sometimes self-employment had been a later career option and an occupational pension had been built up in a previous job. Earnings from self-employment among these respondents were not especially high.

On leaving work, none of this group had a pension immediately. They waited until they reached state pension age to draw their pension, either because they were obliged to do so, or because they felt it would make sense financially. They managed in the interim period by living on savings, on benefits, or from the income of a partner. They generally felt anxious about their financial situation, apart from one woman who had already reached pension age, and had two small private pensions to draw on, in addition to the state pension.

Summary

Given the descriptions in this section of people's circumstances, it seems fairly clear and not surprising that a key influence on people's financial situation is their prior financial circumstances, in particular their earnings and the extent to which they paid into a pension or made long-term savings.

There seems to be more consistency in the situation of people at either end of the income

spectrum than for people on middling incomes. People on low earnings with poor work histories tended to be more likely to have little or no access to private pensions or to savings. If they were saving via a pension the amount was relatively insignificant and became more so following an early departure from work. However, the level of money they received in state benefits could leave them in a situation which was not very different from when they were earning, especially where housing costs were accounted for. In contrast, people on high earnings were in a comfortable position where they had a good level of income from pensions and/or savings, and where housing costs were usually insignificant or paid off.

For people on earnings in between these two ends of the spectrum, factors such as debt and housing costs could make a big difference to their situation when they moved out of work. Financial contributions from women could also make a significant difference to overall household earnings and savings, and sometimes also to pensions. Levels of income from pensions and savings were shaped by prior earnings but also by attitude towards financial preparation for the future. When pension levels were relatively low this left people financially vulnerable when they left work early, and for some people meant managing on low finances for a period until they could draw a full pension.

Managing financial transitions

One of the first decisions that many people had to deal with on retiring was how and when to draw any private pension they had, and then what to do with their pension or redundancy lump sum. People also needed to decide whether to claim disability benefits, although only one person decided against doing this, saying that he thought his savings level would be too high, but also feeling uncomfortable about claiming benefits.

Making the transition from earnings onto benefits was particularly difficult for people. In addition to the drop in income, the process was described as confusing, degrading and unpredictable, and in many cases, there had been delays of up to a couple of months before their money had come through. People also experienced delays in getting redundancy money (but rarely pension money). The result of delays was particularly hard for people moving onto benefits, as it was unusual for them to have any significant savings to fall back on. Delays could therefore mean using up all their savings, or going into debt. Without knowing the level of benefit they were likely to eventually receive, it made it very difficult to know how to budget in the interim period. Changes to benefits received often appeared to happen in an ad hoc way, and as the result of a chance piece of advice. As a result a number of people felt strongly that the Benefits Agency was not sufficiently proactive about informing people of their entitlement.

Not everyone chose to take their pension immediately on leaving work: this was shaped largely by whether they were retiring onto a specific early retirement package offered by work. But it was also shaped by the extent to which they felt it important to defer claiming their pension in order to maximise how much they would be entitled to, and whether they had other sources of income that they could live on for an interim period. Some people deferred buying an annuity if they felt they could manage without it in order to wait for better annuity rates. A few people had to wait until they were 60 due to the rules of their occupational pension.

Managing capital sums

For people who had a lump sum payment of some sort at the point they left work, this was a demarcation point in terms of their financial situation. This was because of the effect the capital lump sum could have on income whereby:

- the lump sum was often used to pay off the remains of a mortgage or buy a property outright, therefore reducing outgoings; and/or
- the lump sum was invested, which could generate future income.

In addition, having a lump sum was a trigger for people to think about their financial future, and often to seek financial advice about investment or managing their money. Lump sums from pensions tended to be used in these ways rather than spent, although parts of them were sometimes spent on getting a new car, having work done on the house, buying a holiday home, or having a special holiday.

Redundancy lump sums tended to be smaller amounts than pension lump sums, and tended therefore to be spent in total on household expenditure, for example, purchases of large items, such as a car, or redecoration, or paying off bills or debts. For people on lower incomes, this was a form of investment in terms of putting money into concrete things now that would result in less need for expenditure at a later stage when they had less income. One man purchased a freezer so that he could then buy more cheaply in bulk and freeze things for the future. For people on means-tested benefits there was an incentive to use up their lump sum in order to keep themselves below the savings threshold. This was something people tended to be quite aware of, and in fact had used a number of ways to get around this rule: one man had paid the lump sum over to his sister, and she had given him regular amounts of income in return until the lump sum was used up.

People receiving a private pension tended to have a decision to make about how much of their pension they would take as a lump sum and how much as payments. It was very common for people to say they wanted to take the maximum lump sum they could. Only two respondents, who had both received financial advice, decided to take lower lump sums than they were offered; one did so in order to purchase an additional five years of pension contributions and the other did so in order to maximise the amount of pension payments his wife would get if he were to die first.

The reason given for taking the maximum lump sum was that it would maximise the amount of money they had access to and control over now, and would be financially worthwhile if they were to die relatively soon. It appeared to be received wisdom that this was the sensible path, and some people knew of calculations that had been done showing at what stage you would have to die in order for it to be a financial advantage:

"Well you're working class, you've never had a lot of money, you've paid into this system and all of a sudden you get the opportunity of having a lump sum ... some people would think well it's as good as like a footballs win on the pools. And you think 'Well what shall I do?', it's a risk you've got to take. You can think to yourself 'I might die next year' so I'll have a lump sum, at least I've got something in hand. Or I'll have the bigger pension and if I live longer than seven years I'm quids in…. I think it's seven years or it might be even less than that, little bit less than that … but you can't work out how long you're going to live, you can't say can you?" (male, was a police officer, left work aged 52, received pension lump sum of £50,000 and annual pension income of £13,000)

A slightly different reason for choosing a maximum lump sum over maximising income was in order to keep the money as capital (as future security) and not spend it all as income. People had various things in mind for using their lump sum payment, the most common of which was to purchase property or pay off the mortgage. The desire to pay off the mortgage was driven less by calculations about their future financial situation, and more by an emotional response to be relieved of the burden of the mortgage debt:

"I hated the damned thing from the moment I took it out, I couldn't stand the idea of being in hock to some faceless bureaucracy, so I just – as soon as I got the money I just went round and paid it off – just didn't want the idea of a mortgage, you know – that was the very first thing I did with, with the cash." (male, was a lecturer, left work aged 52, received pension lump sum of £30,000 and pension income of £12,000 a year)

Managing on a reduced income

The main decision that most people needed to make about their post-retirement money was how to manage on a reduced income. As described in Chapter 5, not everyone felt that their income was much reduced, especially by the time they took into account that their spending had also reduced. This was true of people on high pensions and people who had been low earners, as their post-retirement income was not very different from their income in work. Some people had significantly reduced income, but this was compensated by having high levels of savings or investments, which could be used to generate income. For the remainder, living on a reduced income forced changes in lifestyle and ways of managing money.

Absolute amounts of money were significant here, as well as amounts of income relative to earnings. For example, where an individual or a couple were still able to pay their basic food and housing and utility bills, then adjusting to a reduced income meant cutting back a little on clothes, going out, petrol, holidays and 'luxuries'. This was something that many people felt they would be doing anyway having stopped work and feeling less desire to go out. Outgoings were reduced around this time because of a reduced mortgage and children leaving home. At the same time, people talked about having longer amounts of time to shop around for the best deals.

People living on low incomes had to use new strategies to manage their money in order to make it stretch further to meet essential needs, and it was acknowledged that some costs could also go up when having more free time or time at home, such as heating, the telephone bill, or the food bill. People used methods to prioritise their spending (for example, by always paying bills first, then food, then spending what was left), or to spread their costs (for example, by buying in bulk, or by paying fixed weekly amounts on bills). Housing costs were a significant expense for some people, where they still had a mortgage or were not eligible for full Housing Benefit. However, people on low incomes were, not surprisingly, nervous and wary of borrowing, especially among people who had previous bad experiences of debt.

Money management between couples

Given the transitions that individuals were making between a work and a home role, it is possible that they were also changing the roles that they played in relation to their money, particularly when the source of that money had shifted. However, among the respondents in this study the predominant pattern was one of continuity between the husband and wife in terms of roles in money management. Roles were shaped by a (usually tacit) agreement between the couple that was either based on a principle of a joint or 'partnership' approach, or that drew on what were described as the relative skills of each partner whereby:

- just one partner was in charge of financial decisions and budgeting; or
- there was a division of labour, typically that the wife managed the day-to-day budgeting, and the husband had the control over the financial planning, including pensions and investments.

Interviews with both partners confirmed these roles, and they appeared to be firmly held, perhaps because by this stage of life, partners had often been together for 25 years or more. A small number of the interviews hinted that the husbands who had worked in professional occupations were more involved, and more controlling, of finances following their retirement. This was partly linked to having more time to become involved, but was also perhaps a way of maintaining a management role.

There was some evidence of an awareness that moving into retirement could increase the dependency of one partner on the other, given the reduced opportunity to earn an independent income, and the lost opportunity to build up any pension. This was not strongly articulated but lay beneath the surface of the way some people described their finances. For example, one woman (who had been the breadwinner for some years) talked about her husband looking forward to getting 'his own' pension. Several women said they regretted deciding not to make National Insurance or pension contributions during the time they were working. The implications for the dependent partner who might find themselves on their own were clear from the concern expressed by many that they had made sure their pension would continue paying out after their death, and relatively high levels of anxiety about financial planning demonstrated by women who were widowed. One man had deliberately set up a bank account on behalf of his wife in the hope that she would become more financially astute and self-sufficient for when he might no longer be around to help.

The role of financial advice

If people sought financial advice at all, it tended to be at the point immediately leading up to leaving work and in relation to managing post-retirement income. Advice therefore tended to come too late to help with lifetime financial planning, although could help with managing day-to-day budgeting or debt among people on low incomes, or future financial planning given retirement resources (see pages 32-34). Courses run by employers had been helpful for people who might not otherwise have sought advice. Views of the advice received tended to be shaped, of course, by whether the recommended path had worked out well or not.

There was a general feeling that it can be very hard to know how best to manage finances most effectively in a complex and unpredictable environment, and some people applied this not only to themselves but also to financial advisers. In fact, some people felt deeply suspicious of advisers' ability to make good decisions and to act independently, and they were more comfortable acting on their own judgement and knowledge. Different levels of confidence in financial matters generally affected people's ability to access and engage with financial advisers. Advice from family and friends was also valued, as was learning from other people's good, and particularly, bad, experiences.

Conclusions

Some retirement pathways appear more likely to lead to impoverished circumstances and financially vulnerable situations. The two main negative factors in this study were an unplanned and abrupt departure from work, combined with a prior work history that had not allowed an opportunity to build up a reasonable occupational or private pension. Starting a private pension too late had in retrospect proved to be a high risk for people with this combination of circumstances. Although past earnings level was key in being able to build up a retirement income, a proactive approach towards saving for the future could help significantly. The type of pension scheme available to someone through their work also made a difference. Married or previously married women were potentially vulnerable as they were far less likely to have built up their own pension rights.

People who had low to average earnings during their lifetime and faced restricted options when deciding about leaving work found themselves having to make difficult decisions, and this affected their future financial situation. For some it simply meant expecting to spend the rest of their life dependent on state benefits and state pension. If they had a private pension but it was not sufficiently large to draw at the point they retired, they were placed in a very difficult period of having to wait for a number of years. This group were perhaps the worst off in terms of adjusting to and managing a financial transition, given a reduced interim income, a high level of uncertainty about the future, and perhaps needing to use up critical savings. People who initiated their retirement themselves, rather than taking up a work offer of an 'early retirement' route, were also potentially vulnerable, especially if their plans were based around drawing income from potentially unreliable investments.

In terms of this research study, it is too early to assess how the different ways that people managed their money might affect their longer-term financial situation. Certainly, some people were already regretting making investments in some areas, and had shifted their investment strategy as a result, for example out of stock market investment and into lower risk areas. What is clear is that people who had neither a reasonable income nor reasonable savings (around £10,000 per annum, and at least the same amount in savings), found it far more difficult to manage their financial lives. This was because they had no 'safety net' of savings if anything went wrong, and any small amounts of lump sum that they did receive or save could easily get used up on supplementing their daily living.

5

Living with early retirement: attitudes and rationales

Introduction

This chapter describes how people feel about their financial situation now and in the future, and the attitudes and rationales that underpin financial decisions and action that they take once retired. It covers why people feel the way they do about their financial situation, and what people consider to be important in terms of current and future spending and saving. It builds on some of the attitudes already described in Chapter 4, for example approach towards money management and planning, and more specifically people's attitudes towards managing a lump sum payment on retirement (see pages 28-9).

What do people think about their situation?

As well as providing an objective description of people's financial situations following their early withdrawal from work, it was important in the research study to understand how people felt subjectively about their situation. There are a number of qualifying points when looking at these subjective assessments. It is well known that people adjust their spending in order to live within their means, and therefore we might expect some lack of consciousness of how their financial situation has changed. Also, people who may feel comfortable with their finances now, are not in a position to say how they might feel about their finances in the future.

Views about finances also appeared to be influenced by how people felt about their life generally having left work. Where leaving work had been a positive choice, with a view to taking on alternative roles such as voluntary work, or enjoying active leisure time, then the issue of finances often appeared to fade into the background, provided of course, that people were not living in poverty. Where the decision to leave work had been made in a hurry, in negative circumstances, or where it had been forced on people, then there was not the same level of comfort about their situation, at least not initially. Here, finances could dominate people's thoughts. However, where people's personal circumstances were extremely difficult, finances were sometimes the least of their worries.

Views among people on low incomes

There was an absolute level of income, below which people generally felt that they were living in very difficult circumstances; this was around £150 a week for an individual, and around £200 a week for a couple. These are just approximate figures, based on the feelings and views of people living on these types of incomes (people were not asked to state an amount of disposable income that was manageable or not), and clearly the weekly amounts will result in different circumstances depending on a household's outgoings or different needs.

Among people who were on this income level following their retirement, attitudes can be arranged along a spectrum, as shown in Figure 5.1.

Figure 5.1: Attitudes towards financial situation among people on low incomes

Untroubled	Resigned	Angry/upset

◀─────────────────────────────▶

It was unusual for people to not feel troubled about having very little money, and it tended to arise in situations where there had been traumatic personal circumstances, although the individuals did describe it as part of their ongoing attitude towards money:

"Money was no real concern, no, money's never really been part of my life ... so again it didn't really matter. Because it was such a vast change of life it's literally a new life, you know. I absolutely started ... I was 58 then and I started with not a penny. So you've got to start all again at that age from nowhere, which is a bit of a challenge." (male, separated, was a taxi driver, left work aged 58, received Income Support)

Far more typical was a feeling of resignation or stoicism in the light of financial difficulties. Here people's resignation was underpinned by two different rationales, linked partly to whether their retirement income was similar to or less than their income from work:

- they could not see how things could have been different, and their expectations had been and continued to be low; poverty in retirement was a continuation of a lifetime of low income;
- they felt they had adjusted to their reduced circumstances, and were able to live on the money they had, even if it was very little, because their needs were less than they used to be.

People on low retirement incomes also made a number of trade-offs in reconciling themselves to their situation, whereby money was given a low priority relative to other things in their lives. This was especially true where the circumstances of retirement involved ill-health or leaving what had been a very stressful and demanding job. Having emotional and physical health was highly valued, as was being able to spend time with a partner or family. This echoes the dominance of personal reasons over financial reasons given by people at the time of retiring (see Chapter 3). It was also common to compare their own financial situation favourably to what they knew of other people's situations, and to difficult financial times in their own past, particularly in early married life with young children.

The people who felt upset or angry about their situation tended to be people who felt they should have done more about their situation, either that they should have looked harder at staying on at work, perhaps doing part-time work or a different role at work, or that they should have planned more for their financial future. They tended to have been on slightly higher earnings than people who were more resigned to their situation and therefore the change in income was felt as a more significant drop:

"I try not to let it dwell on my mind but like most people when you're laying in bed at night and everything is going through your mind and you can't get to sleep 'cos it's all – and that's when you think about it. You think 'oh God am I going to get through this week'. I don't know there's just 101 things that go through your head, you think 'what if so and so happened'." (female, was an ambulance worker, left work aged 48, had no retirement income of her own, husband was still working)

However, the difference in where people fell on the spectrum also reflected a straightforward difference in approach to money and how significant it was in people's lives compared to other things. In addition, women in this study were often more anxious about money than men.

Views among people on higher incomes

As discussed in Chapter 3, people on higher incomes who chose to leave work usually had a fairly clear idea of what their immediate financial situation was going to be before they did so, and so it was unusual for people to say they had been surprised or disappointed to find themselves in the financial situation they were in. When it came to anticipated amounts of a future pension, people generally recognised that they had little idea of what to expect, and in that sense were not likely to be surprised, either pleasantly or unpleasantly, when it came into payment:

"What's your pension going to be? You don't know. I've sent off for a [frozen occupational] pension prediction but it's still not real, this is part of the airy fairy stuff that I was saying. Until you've got it in your pocket you don't really know what it is…. With the present state of the economy you don't really know whether those figures you've got in your head will actually materialise." (male, was an engineer, left work aged 61, no retirement income of own at the time, wife had pension lump sum of £46,000 plus annual income of £15,000)

Having a pension forecast some time previously could, however, lead to disappointment when it came into payment if the pension value of the fund had reduced relative to the time when the forecast was made.

People were sometimes caught out in two different types of unanticipated scenario:

- where investments had done less well than expected: (i) an endowment policy that did not generate sufficient cash to pay off the mortgage and left one couple with a shortfall of several thousand pounds, or (ii) investments dropped in value, and resulted in lower levels of investment income (significant for people whose retirement plan involved heavy reliance on investment income); and
- where their personal circumstances changed in an unpredictable way after retirement: one couple ended up selling their house and purchasing a larger house in order that their parents could live with them; this involved them in greater financial commitment and expense than they had expected.

There were also people who felt that they were not as well off as they would ideally have liked to have been in their retirement, and had a number of regrets about the way they had planned their pension or managed their retirement:

- some women, especially those in more difficult circumstances, felt angry that they had not paid money into their own pension during their working lives, and that they were now dependent on state support or on a low pension from their husband;
- if investments had been set up to mature at retirement age, then this sometimes meant living with less income temporarily until the policy matured;
- a small number of people felt they had not looked sufficiently carefully at their financial situation, what they needed to live on, prior to

retiring, and found that they were finding it harder than they had expected;
- there were some regrets that decisions made at the time of retirement had not been the best in retrospect: for example, a decision not to pay off the whole mortgage, or an investment decision that was taken too quickly and had not reaped good rewards;
- a number of people felt they had not invested their money in the best way in the past; this was shaped by how they saw relative investments performing, for example, they now felt they should have invested more in property, or in stocks or shares, or in PEPs. They felt they had not known enough about the relative merits of different investments to make the best decision.

On the other hand, however, a number of people felt things had worked out better than they had expected, partly if they had received higher income or some extra money that was unanticipated. Several people had inherited money and this had helped their financial situation; others had found that savings and investments had grown more, not less, than they had expected or realised. There was also an element of adaptation involved: after initial anxiety about reducing their income, they had realised that they could in fact live fairly well on the amount they had. There was some surprise at how the amount of money they needed to spend had gone down since leaving work: children were no longer living at home, and there was less need to save now that there was a permanent income from a pension. In addition, living on a reduced income was also easier for people if (i) it was only for a relatively short period until standard retirement age, and (ii) people knew that they had savings they could draw on for larger actual or potential expenses.

Planning for the future

The previous section has started to set out some of the ways that people thought about money post-retirement. People's feelings about their financial situation were shaped partly by the amount of financial resource they had, both absolute and relative to their previous income from work. Feelings were also shaped by overall attitudes towards money in relation to other priorities, prior expectations, and feelings that they had made mistakes or taken a wrong course.

This section looks at how people were planning for their future financially, and the rationales that lay behind this planning.

As in the previous section, it is helpful to divide the respondents into two groups, given the very different situations people are in following their withdrawal from work: (i) people who are mainly reliant on state benefits, and (ii) people who have income from other sources, particularly from private pensions.

Financial planning when living on state benefits

This group of people were mainly dependent on state benefits following their withdrawal from work. One or two had a small private pension in payment or to come (that is, up to around £4,000 annual income). They generally had no savings other than an emergency reserve of a few hundred pounds, or a similar amount saved up for short-term purchases or holidays. A couple of households had a slightly higher level of savings in tax-efficient savings policies.

In part, the lack of savings reflected the inability to save on very low levels of income, both currently and in the past from earnings. It also reflected the disincentive to save among people on means-tested benefits, where savings levels above the savings threshold would mean withdrawal of benefits. Among this group, there may have been a longer-term attitude that saving was not important, although it was not possible to distinguish this from people's statements that they had never had enough money to save.

There was therefore a more or less complete lack of any financial planning for the future among this group. People were just living on a week-by-week basis, managing their money as best they could. Among people with serious or terminal illnesses there was some pessimism about how long they might live; if they had no partner to worry about they sought to enjoy the present rather than plan for the future. Avoiding debt was a common and strongly held objective, and financial aspirations were low. People acknowledged that they found it very hard to think ahead to the future, and there was a

general anxiety about how things would change at state pension age. It was very rare that anyone had any sense of certainty about how much state pension they would be entitled to, and how that would affect other benefits:

"I really don't know anything about pensions, and that's the truth, I don't know whether when I'm 60 I will be, I don't think I'll be entitled to a pension if I'm not working, I think I'll be entitled to Income Support because I don't think Incapacity goes past 60. I think at 60 it all changes. I really don't know what I get when I get to 60. I'm half frightened to find out because I really don't know." (female, divorced, was a care assistant, left work aged 48, received disability benefits)

No one mentioned the Minimum Income Guarantee, and there was a fairly common assumption that they would be worse off when reaching retirement age because they would lose disability benefits and means-tested benefits (especially if they had a small private pension to come). There was also confusion about how having a small private pension might affect eligibility for the state pension:

"... the more I think about it [her private pension] the less I think it's important. Because I get a pension now seeing I'm pension age, and if that was to come into place say in the next year that is all I'm sure I would get. I'm sure the government would take the pension I'm getting away." (female, divorced, was a nurse, left work aged 55, received disability benefits)

People generally expected private pensions to be very low, partly because they had not been able to make full contributions up until retirement age.

In one case, a couple were pinning all their hopes on the point in two years' time when the husband reached 65 and was able to claim his private pension. Their aspirations for that point were relatively low compared to others in the study – to pay off the mortgage, to buy some new furniture and to start going out again at weekends. They were struggling enormously with getting by during the interim period, which had already lasted 10 years, surviving on the husband's Incapacity Benefit. They had not had his pension fund valued since he had left work 10 years ago, when it was valued at £12,000. It seems unlikely that this would generate an income much higher than their current income, and that they would probably be disappointed:

> "We know this money's coming at 65, but it's – you don't want to wish your life away, but this is the only thing that really keeps us going, 'cos you can say to yourself, well, god spare us, if we both – and I hope that we both manage to get to 65 – that we will be far better, 'cos the mortgage will be finished next year – and this is the only thing that keeps you on." (female, was a shop assistant, left work aged 60, received state pension, and husband's disability benefits)

People who owned their own homes were struggling with paying mortgages still, but valued the fact that they would have the financial security of a house, and for some, they felt glad they would have something to leave to their children when they died (see below for discussion of attitudes towards homes and towards inheritance). At the same time, living in local authority housing provided security for some people, with the knowledge that they would not have to pay any expenses if something went wrong.

The one area that people in this group had planned for was after they died. Several people had life insurance policies, which they hoped would pay out small amounts to cover their funeral costs, and possibly leave some additional money for a son or daughter. One man had arranged his private pension, so that he took a very small lump sum and his wife would get higher-level payments as a result after he died.

People with incomes from private pensions

This group of people had (or knew they had coming within a few years) pension incomes ranging from around £6,000 a year to over £40,000 a year – it is therefore a diverse group. In addition to having higher levels of income than people who were largely dependent on state benefits, their situation is distinct from the previous group in that they also had savings, in part through having received a pension lump sum payment.

After withdrawing from work, people were generally not expecting their income situation to change significantly. Some still had a private pension to draw when they reached standard retirement age, and of course, all would receive the state pension. Among people on annual pension incomes of less than £20,000, the state pension was expected to be a bonus, something that would enable them to buy some extras; where pension income was higher than this, the state pension was not expected to make much difference. Occasionally, the condition for taking an early private pension was that it would reduce by the amount of the state pension, once the latter was drawn.

People could feel anxious about their future situation if they were unsure about whether their private pensions would keep up with rises in the cost of living; some people seemed to make an assumption about this without knowing for sure. Similarly, being mainly reliant on investment growth or income could make people feel uncertain about their finances compared to receiving regular income from earnings:

> "I find that very difficult to comprehend really that there is money coming in but it's not at the end of each month and it's not a certain amount so I think that's probably what makes me panic slightly, because you're used to a regular pay packet coming in…. It's because I don't see that amount in a little statement or a cash book each month, it's in an ISA which is somewhere else and not accessible and not in front of me." (female, was a secretary, left work aged 46, no retirement income of her own, husband was still working, then left work with £30,000 redundancy lump sum and investment income of £15,000 per year)

In terms of capital, some people were expecting things to change at a point when they paid off their mortgage, or when a policy matured. There was an indication that this might mean disappointment in a few cases, where investments were not doing as well as initially assumed. People often knew that they may inherit some money when a parent died, but it was common for people to say that they were not relying on this, in part because they knew it might get used up, for example, paying for long-term care.

Objectives for financial future

There were two main things that people in this group generally wanted to achieve with their money once they had left work:

- a regular, guaranteed income: this could be from a pension and/or from income generated from investments. However, being reliant on investment income had to be planned well, and could lead to a greater sense of anxiety;
- some capital as a security for the short- and long-term future: this could mean savings accounts or policies, or longer-term investments, or equity in their house.

Given these two broad goals, how people made decisions about their finances was then influenced primarily by their approach towards spending versus saving at this stage in their life. There seemed to be little difference between husbands and wives in their underlying approach. Decisions appeared to have been taken jointly, or led by one partner but happily accepted by the other, in the belief that one partner was far more qualified to deal with financial matters. There were some slight differences in strength of feeling about aspects of finances, for example leaving money to children (see below), but on the whole the impression given was of discussion and evolution of a joint approach.

Spending versus saving: different rationales

The area where there was most variation between couples was on the question of spending money now versus saving for the future. In part, the variation is explained by different levels of income and capital (for example, where capital and income are both relatively high, it is easier to decide to spend more now and worry less about the future), but another element of the explanation lies in people's beliefs about saving, shaped by, among other things, long-term habit and parental attitudes.

- Continuing to preserve savings, at the cost of having spending money available now, made sense for people who did not feel entirely confident financially, and who also felt that they did not want large disposable incomes at this stage in their lives; their financial

aspirations were low, and caution with regard to the future was more significant:

> "Because we can manage without we might as well make the savings work as hard as possible by, you know accumulating rather than take it out now because we don't really need it at the moment." (male, was a technical manager, left work aged 61, received redundancy and pension lump sums totalling £25,000 and pension income of £3,000 a year)

- Others said that they were starting to shift the balance from saving towards spending, or at least towards having savings in a form that was more easily accessible. People were keen to enjoy life, and being able to have holidays (although not necessarily expensive holidays) was a common feature of people's aspirations:

> "I think it's a problem, it's trying to hit the happy medium ... what's the point, scrimping and scrounging, coping, you know, and waiting for something that might never happen – and yet on the other hand, you know, people live to be 90, don't they – it's trying to hit that happy sort of middle of the road situation, where you're enjoying – 'cos I feel that we're sort of at this active age of retirement and I think – I say, well, we should do these things." (female, was a teacher, left work aged 53, received pension lump sum plus income of £7,000 a year)

This latter group of people did not necessarily have higher levels of income or capital than the previous group, just a different approach to their finances. In taking this approach, some people were conscious that they were going against standard financial advice, but felt this was the right decision for them:

> "It was very difficult to get him [financial adviser] to understand what our needs were, which were a lot simpler than his needs.... He still wants us to go on saving and saving and we think 'Well why?'. You know if we've got this now and we've got an income, what do we need to keep on saving for?.... I mean I found we had to keep saying 'But we don't want that', we

don't want at this moment in time to go on world cruises, we don't want a bigger house because our needs are actually less." (female, was a teacher, left work aged 60, received pension lump sum of £45,000 and annual income of £15,000)

Objectives for long-term saving

On the whole, people were not saving with anything specific in mind. However, a few respondents articulated a more specifically planned approach to their finances: perhaps not surprisingly, they tended to be people who had ongoing contact with a financial adviser. They had taken certain considerations into account when deciding about their finances (for example, that their family tended to be long-living, or that they wanted to help their children buy property, or knew that they would have to pay for healthcare in the future), and had organised finances accordingly. One man had taken out a 20-year insurance policy when he retired in order to generate future funds. Looking at life beyond 70 (still 10-15 years away for this group) appeared to be a significant psychological future point of focus. These people had not necessarily done anything significantly different with their money, but perhaps were just expressing their choices with more of a strategy in mind.

Apart from these proactive planners, people adopted a more broad-brush approach. They felt that having some money invested gave them general security about their future in relation to unknown one-off large expenditures, for example that they might be able to afford to have private health treatment, or that they would like to have some money to leave their children (see below). On the whole, people did not mention thinking about saving for long-term care, or said they were deliberately not thinking that far ahead. Where people had thought about it, it was more with concern at feeling unable to do much about it, or not believing that care plans on offer would actually cover them for what they might want:

"I ought to spend some time thinking about private health and all the rest of it, the state so far has been good for us, but when you read about the problems, and packing people off to France for medical care – if I was sensible and thinking ahead, I ought to

think of severe old age and what's the provision for that, but I prefer not to for a bit, I might have got 10 or 15 good years – and let's spend the money while we – while it's coming in." (male, was a teacher, left work aged 55, received pension lump sum and annual income of £11,000)

There was a common feeling that it was very hard to plan for an unpredictable future, but that having some money invested would be helpful whatever came up:

"[My approach is] I've got a chunk of money, how am I gonna get the best return from that chunk of money..... We've never done long-term planning like that because you never know what's gonna come round the corner." (male, was a company director, left work aged 55, received redundancy lump sum of £30,000 and annual investment income of £15,000)

Equity in their own home, like savings, provided a strong sense of general financial security: it was (i) a guarantee of somewhere to live, and (ii) a fall-back option to sell the home if it became financially necessary. No one talked about trading down their home as a fixed plan in order to realise capital – it was seen only as a last resort; this was linked to the emotional attachment people had to their homes, driven by having spent a long time there and having invested effort in making it their home. Only a few people had a less strong attachment to their home, and said they would not mind selling their home if it meant they could do something else, or as an alternative to going back to work.

Linked to this emotional, rather than financial, view of the home, people were also keen to pay off mortgages, although occasionally people took a more financial view, and had calculated that it made more financial sense to keep a small mortgage going.

Views about leaving money after death varied enormously. It tended to be an important consideration to make sure that a partner would be well provided for if the main pension holder died. This was generally part of the rules of their pension scheme. Leaving capital for descendants was very important for some, but far less so for others. People's views tended to be shaped by their parents' views, in part by how much help the respondents had received themselves from their parents: this could work to encourage them to want to do the same, or occasionally the opposite.

"... [father's] philosophy was that your children should be better off than you, and that's how it should go. So we were very lucky in that I think my grandparents helped when my parents bought their house, they helped them out with a deposit. If my mother and father hadn't given us the deposit for our first house we would never have had one, so it's a knock-on effect. Any savings, any money that I have now that was inherited hopefully I will help my daughter." (female, was a secretary, left work aged 43, received disability benefits, husband was still working, when left work received pension and lump sum totalling £90,000 and annual pension income of £9,000)

"... his [father's] philosophy was that – I've made my life and this is my money, now it's up to you to go off and – I had to work for my money, you've got to go and work for your own. And that was his philosophy. And I suppose it's my philosophy in a way. Although having said that he will be well provided for, better than most I would think." (male, was a company director, left work aged 55, received redundancy lump sum of £30,000 and annual investment income of £15,000)

Many people adopted a pragmatic, rather than principled, position somewhere in the middle: they would not stint themselves in order to leave money for their children, but neither would they not leave them anything, if they had a choice. Opinions were shaped by how much they felt their children needed helping, with some respondents commenting that their children were in more expensive homes than they were. The view was occasionally expressed that Inheritance Tax was a disincentive to passing money onto children – it was better to spend it themselves. As before, the house was seen as the final fall-back asset – it was something that their children would have even if there were no other savings left. However, the fact that this might not be available if they had to sell their home to release capital was not really acknowledged (despite an awareness that such a situation affected their

own likelihood of inheritance). People's responses suggested that they may have felt it was too early to be planning for what they might leave to children when they may still have many years of expenditure, some of it unpredictable, themselves.

Conclusions

People generally found it very hard to think and therefore plan in any specific way for future eventualities, and there appeared to be little consideration of the fact that, having retired early, this group may find themselves with 10 years or so additional time having to finance retirement than they might have expected. This was partly because people were operating with limited amounts of money, and tended to prioritise spending their income rather than using it for ongoing future planning and further saving at this stage. Among people on very low incomes, planning for the future was not an option – they were managing on a week-by-week basis. However, the lack of planning was also underpinned by the difficulty in thinking ahead to what might happen, when there could be any number of unpredictable, intervening events. In this context, many people's response was to feel that it made sense for them to spend their income rather than save it.

There were two things that enabled people to feel a sense of financial security about the future: first, having a guaranteed fixed pension income that was enough to fund necessities and at least some extras, and second, having some savings and a house that they owned outright. The house in particular provided a critical safety net. Without these things, people were more likely to feel vulnerable and out of control of their finances.

People's feelings about their financial situation were underpinned partly by their prior expectations but also by the extent to which they felt they had made an informed choice, both at the point of retirement and earlier in their lives when planning for retirement. Some people felt they had made mistakes in not planning finances appropriately when they were younger or that they had made rushed and poor decisions about their money at the time of retirement.

Finances were, however, not necessarily of primary importance in people's lives, and some people were pleasantly surprised at their ability to manage on lower incomes. Where leaving work had been linked to difficult circumstances, and/or fears over health, then having their health and having time out of work to enjoy life tended to dominate people's feelings. However, these people were still all within 10 years of having left work, and further research would be needed to see if people feel similarly once they are 10 or 20 years into retirement.

6

Conclusions and policy implications

Introduction

This research set out to address questions surrounding the role of financial factors in people's moves out of work and into early retirement. In doing so, the research has covered a wide range of areas: the process of and decision around leaving work, the financial implications of moving out of work, and people's attitudes towards managing and planning their finances, in the context of an early move out of work.

As a piece of exploratory qualitative research, one of the primary objectives of this report has been to describe the range and diversity of people's experience and views. Diversity of circumstance and experience has been particularly evident among the group of people covered by this study, and the heterogeneous nature of the group does not lend itself to drawing out a straightforward set of conclusions or implications for policy.

The dimensions that appear to be central in framing people's experiences are first, the degree of choice and control they experience on moving out of work and towards retirement, and second, their financial circumstances during their working life (for example, their income from earnings, access to occupational pension, and accumulation of personal savings in different forms). People who move out of work before state pension age range from either end of these two dimensions: total choice and control over circumstances to no choice and control, people in very high income brackets to people on low levels of state benefit. Perhaps not surprisingly, the findings suggest that on the whole, but not always, people in strong financial and occupational situations have greater choice and control over leaving work and arranging their

finances subsequently, although further research would be needed to test the strength of this relationship.

A further factor that has considerable bearing on people's experiences is the nature of any impairment or health problem they have, especially among people who are in a less strong occupational and financial situation.

The policy implications here will primarily focus on the groups and sets of circumstances that the research identifies as potentially most vulnerable given an early move out of work. These are people who have not built up a reasonable retirement income, through personal or occupational pension schemes, and who have little in the way of additional savings or investment policies. The research suggests that the people most likely to be in this situation are:

- people on low or modest incomes from earnings;
- people with periods out of work;
- people who have little choice about leaving work (for example, due to redundancy or disability);
- women who have no pension rights in their own name.

The implications for policy of the research findings are drawn out as follows in two main areas: employment policy and personal finances.

Implications for employment policy

Financial factors seem to play a relatively low key role in people's motivations to leave work. Personal factors such as concerns about health or a desire to have personal rather than work time, and/or a wish to get out of an unpleasant job dominate the reasons people give for leaving work. Financial considerations primarily play a role in terms of providing the framework within which people make their decision, a determination of whether leaving work is affordable, if there is a choice.

However, choices about moving out of work are often very restricted, especially in circumstances of redundancy and/or disability. In these cases, people in their fifties and early sixties may have little or no choice about leaving their job, and can then find it difficult and increasingly dispiriting trying to find other paid employment. This research suggests that after one to two years of searching, people seem to abandon hope. The difficulty in finding and securing an appropriate job (given for some people the existence of an impairment or health condition) combined with actual or perceived disincentives within the benefit system (due in part to low awareness of benefits), discourages people from looking for work for any length of time when they are already close to retirement age. Once out of work, confidence can be damaged and skills become out of date, creating further barriers to returning to work. People in this study felt that they received little in the way of support or advice to help them stay in or return to work, and felt that the way the benefit system treated them (as unlikely to work again) discouraged any attempts to look for work. In addition, some people adjust to the idea of being 'early retired' and consciously trade-off a better financial situation for health and quality of life.

Driven in part by a desire to encourage people to delay drawing pensions and increase opportunities to save, the government has sought to support and encourage older people to return to work through the New Deal programmes, in particular the New Deal 50+ and the New Deal for Disabled People, and has proposed pilot work with voluntary sector organisations to extend information about back-to-work help and local job and volunteering opportunities to people aged 50 and over. New initiatives in the area of in-work benefits, for example, the Working Tax Credit, should help people to be better off returning to work than staying on benefits. At the same time, state pension age is being equalised at 65 for men and women between 2010 and 2020. During this transition and subsequently, both men and women aged between 60 and women's state pension age will

be entitled to the full range of job search support and benefits available through Jobcentre Plus. Further, there have been a number of measures aimed at encouraging employers to recruit (and retain) older workers. The Age Positive campaign encourages employers to remove age discrimination from their employment practices and encourages the use of a flexible and fair retirement policy. It is important, however, that the sorts of jobs on offer should not only be appropriate for people's capacities, but attractive in terms of financial benefit, and maintaining work–life balance.

Given the difficulties of finding other work once a job has been lost, support to help and encourage people to stay with their existing employer is another important area for policy development. This might include considering a change to the nature of a job, working hours or other flexible working arrangements if people wish to review their work–life balance as they approach retirement, while at the same time promoting policies to prevent the development of work-related health conditions. Among disabled people, the government is piloting the Job Retention and Rehabilitation scheme, which will provide a range of personal support measures to people identified as being at risk of losing their job through ill-health or disability. There is also the possibility for people with health or disability problems (under certain eligibility conditions) of moving to part-time work and receiving tax credits to top up their income; this option could be extended to benefit a wider range of people (whether for health reasons or caring responsibilities).

It is clear, however, that there are groups of older people for whom continuing in or finding paid work is not an option, particularly given severe impairment or health conditions. For these people, it is important that financial support prior to reaching state pension age is provided at a level that enables a reasonable standard of living, and which ideally would not mean that people lose out in making contributions towards their pension, including their state second pension or a private pension.

The evidence from this study supports the need for the development of employment policies that allow people to retire at a time and in a way that suits their circumstances. Control and choice over retirement helps people to prepare themselves financially, as well as psychologically. Having the opportunity to move out of work gradually, through, for example, part-time working or other flexible packages, rather than with an abrupt unwanted departure, would help some people with managing this transition. Recent proposals to allow people to continue working in a reduced capacity for their existing employer once they have already started drawing their occupational pension should enable a more gradual transition out of work (DWP/HM Treasury/Inland Revenue, 2002).

The government, in its recent Green Paper, has also started to look at ways of making early retirement less financially attractive, for example, by increasing the age at which people can start drawing from a private pension, and the age at which public sector employees can receive a full pension. However, the research strongly suggests that personal factors can be as important to people as financial considerations, if not more so. Women appear to be more likely than men to leave work early on the basis of personal reasons, seeking to retire alongside their partners. It should not therefore be surprising that some people will choose to leave work early regardless of whether they would be better off if they had stayed in work longer, and despite policies that might seek to encourage them to work for longer.

Implications for personal finances

The degree of choice and control over leaving work, as well as people's prior financial circumstances, appears to shape the sorts of financial situations that people find themselves in on moving out of work. Where people had the opportunity to make a considered decision, they generally did so with sufficient information about their financial situation that they did not find themselves in an unexpected position once they had left work. Having the choice to draw an occupational pension immediately on retiring, as well as shaping the timing of retirement to coincide with maturation of savings policies, and completion of mortgages, provides people with a secure financial situation. Lack of choice over leaving work can easily result in having to rely on existing savings or on state benefits until a private or state pension can be drawn. Unplanned departures from work can also lead to restricted ability to pay a mortgage, and

interrupted pensions or other saving plans. The group of people on low to average earnings seem from this research to be particularly vulnerable financially to early unplanned departures from paid work. This group may not feel able to save much until they reach their forties or early fifties, so that if they find themselves out of work, they are reliant on incomes substantially lower than their earnings from work. For people who have always been on very low incomes, their financial situation on leaving work may not be very different on benefits compared to their earnings.

Decisions about moving out of work are generally not considered in any detail until relatively close to the point of (early) retirement. These findings echo those from other research that people often leave saving and planning until late in their lives (FSA, 2002). However, by then, the financial situation is already set and people are making decisions given their existing circumstances, rather than setting up how they would ideally have things be. The current study suggests that people's thinking about finances tends to focus on the short to medium term following retirement, rather than on longer-term planning, and on comparative levels of income, rather than on the role of capital or savings. On the whole, people find it difficult to plan for the range of unpredictable events that they may face in the future; this appears to be true of forward planning at the point of retirement, as well as planning for old age during earlier life stages. Policies seeking to help with financial planning should therefore be addressed towards people at different life stages (early planning, pre-retirement and post-retirement).

Saving for the future is particularly difficult when people are in an economically insecure situation, and low levels of savings or contributions to a private pension are particularly vulnerable to an unplanned early exit from work. Women who have not provided for pensions in their own right can find themselves either with a lower joint retirement income than they would otherwise have had, or if they subsequently divorce or their husband dies, may find themselves in a particularly vulnerable financial situation. New regulations for pension sharing on divorce may address this to some extent, but only where pension resources are sufficient to provide adequately for two households rather than one.

Given current concerns about the funding of old age (outlined in Chapter 1), there has been a recent focus on the extent to which people are or are not saving sufficiently for their retirement[4]. The findings from this study suggest that the elements that provide people with a sense of financial security once retired are:

- an income that is guaranteed into the future (ideally an index-linked pension income, rather than income from other sources alone, such as investments); an income that was roughly half their income from earnings appeared to be acceptable to people on average earnings or above;
- a mortgage-free property; and
- some savings for the future.

At this stage, shortly after early retirement, it was unusual for people to have regrets about having made a decision to leave work, at least not financial regrets. However, people did find it hard to look into and plan financially for their future, and it may be that people who are reasonably comfortable at this stage may not be so in 10 or 20 years' time. This could be an area for further research.

Capital in the form of personal savings, as well as an income from pensions, can therefore provide an important security. The government is proposing a range of measures to try to encourage long-term saving (in pensions and other forms) across income groups: among higher earners this takes the form, for example, of the relaxation of the annual limits to the amount people can save in pension schemes, and among people on low incomes, the Pension Credit, introduced in October 2003, is intended to remove disincentives to save for people on state benefits by rewarding people with savings with additional income. It remains to be seen what impact the Pension Credit will have on people's attitudes towards saving. It has been suggested that it could act as a disincentive to save among people on middling incomes who become drawn into means-tested benefits via the Pension Credit for the first time (Emmerson and Wakefield, 2003). In addition, the opportunity to save money during early life in a form that is not

tied up in a pension, and then transfer this into a pension in later life, may encourage more people to save in the knowledge that they can have easy access to the money if they need it; however, it may also discourage pension saving (Emmerson and Wakefield, 2003). New types of pension have been created with a view to giving people with interrupted work histories the opportunity to pay into a pension in a more flexible way – the intention is that this will help people who have traditionally found it difficult to build up a private pension fund. Again, it remains to be seen what impact these will have in practice.

The other main branch of proposed government policy is to improve people's ability to make choices about their future finances, by improving levels of financial awareness. This would take the form of providing everyone with regular statements of their predicted state pension income, and possibly combined statements for all their sources of future pension income. This may well help people to think about whether they want to save more or not for their future, although other calls on resources and difficulty in thinking ahead to what future needs are likely to be may still make it hard for people to plan effectively. The findings from this research suggest a need for improved access to financial information for some groups of people, but also more individually tailored advice at different life stages – in early financial planning, in making decisions about leaving work, and in planning for old age having moved out of work. Areas where it appeared that people could have benefited from more information or advice include:

- planning finances for the future so that they are flexible enough to encompass unknown events such as an early departure from work;
- setting up appropriate and reliable pension schemes given a predicted work history;
- making sound investments;
- preparing for leaving work and assessing precise levels of income and expenditure; having clear pension forecasts;
- better-off calculations to determine how their situation would differ between remaining on benefits or returning to work;
- making decisions about the most appropriate ways of dealing with retirement money, especially lump sum payments;
- working out the likely risk of future events in old age and associated expenditure; and

---

[4] The recent government Green Paper, for example, estimated that around 3 million people were seriously under-saving, or planning to retire too soon (DWP/HM Treasury/Inland Revenue, 2002).

calculating whether and how to prepare for these events.

There may be a particular value in looking at ways of providing advice and information for women, whose lifestyles and therefore pension circumstances tend to sit outside the more 'typical' set of circumstances. At the same time, the situation for women may change as the generation of women who will spend longer periods of their life in paid work, and are more likely to be lone parents, approaches retirement. These groups of women are more likely to have greater experience of financial independence during their working lives compared to the group of women included in this research, and may face a number of different issues in terms of effective planning for the future.

There was, however, evidence of uncertainty about where to go to find financial information and advice, combined with scepticism about the nature of the advice that would be given. Information provision has to therefore be clearly understood, and easily available, and provided through sources that people feel are objective and trustworthy.

Policies to encourage saving for the future need to take into account that, while some people aim to plan their finances effectively in order to retire early, another group of people end up leaving work because they are forced to do so, and are unable to continue an income through earnings. Pension and savings policies also need to address how this group will be best protected when unpredictable events intervene and they are no longer able to follow their original financial plans.

Conclusions

People who have a choice in the timing and circumstances of their retirement not only have the opportunity to do so at a financial time that suits them, but also have the opportunity to make preparations for the transition. This study appears to confirm the findings of a recent Economic and Social Research (ESRC) study that having a choice about leaving work early has a strong influence on people's subsequent quality of life, regardless of their financial circumstances (Blane et al, 2002). This may mean that, even with full financial information, people choose to

be in a situation that is not financially ideal, because it makes sense for them in terms of their priorities when faced with a decision about leaving work. Ideally, policies would seek to address long-term financial planning, rather than decisions around the point of retirement, so that people find themselves in situations where they have more rather than fewer options.

The group of people who have no or very little choice about leaving work early can, however, be in a vulnerable position financially. This group tends to be people who have been in economically less secure positions throughout their lives. Not only are they unable to build up a pension fund or savings any further having left work, but they may have to make use of savings that they have accumulated in order to survive until they can draw a pension. The findings suggest that a range of policies should be aimed at helping this group of people to continue in employment, but where this is not possible, policies should be seeking to protect their financial situation.

References

Banks, J., Blundell, R., Disney, R. and Emmerson, C. (2002) *Retirement, pensions and the adequacy of saving: A guide to the debate*, Briefing Note No 29, London: Institute for Fiscal Studies.

Bardasi, E. and Jenkins, S. (2002) *Income in later life: Work history matters*, Bristol/York: The Policy Press/Joseph Rowntree Foundation.

Barnes, H., Parry, J. and Lakey, J. (2002) *Forging a new future: The experiences and expectations of people leaving paid work over 50*, Bristol/York: The Policy Press/Joseph Rowntree Foundation.

Cabinet Office (2000) *Winning the generation game*, London: Cabinet Office.

Campbell, N. (1999) *The decline of employment among older people in Britain*, CASEPaper 19, London: Centre for the Analysis of Social Exclusion, London School of Economics and Political Science, available at: http://sticerd.lse.ac.uk/case/publications/casepapers.asp

DWP (Department for Work and Pensions)/HM Treasury/Inland Revenue (2002) *Simplicity, security and choice: Working and saving for retirement*, Green Paper, Cm 5677, December, London: DWP.

Emmerson, C. and Wakefield, M. (2003) *Achieving simplicity, security and choice in retirement? An assessment of the government's proposed pension reforms*, Briefing Note No 36, London: Institute for Fiscal Studies.

ESRC (2003) 'Influences on quality of life in early old age', Press release, 17 January.

Evandrou, M. and Glaser, K. (2003) 'Combining work and family life: the pension penalty of caring', *Ageing and Society*, Winter, vol 23, no 5, pp 583-601.

Financial Times (2003) 'Nearly 75% of final salary schemes shut to new entrants', 24 March.

FSA (Financial Services Authority) (2002) *Impact of an ageing population for the FSA*, Consumer Research 10, London: FSA.

Guardian, The (2002) 'Hours of misery', Report of research by Michael White and Stephen Hill for the ESRC's 'Future of work' research programme, 13 November.

Hedges, A. (1998) *Pensions and retirement planning*, DSS Research Report No 83, Leeds: Corporate Document Services.

Lissenburgh, S. and Smeaton, D. (2003) *Employment transitions of older workers: The role of flexible employment in maintaining labour market participation and promoting job quality*, Bristol/York: The Policy Press/Joseph Rowntree Foundation.

Mayhew, V. (2001) *Pensions 2000: Public attitudes to pensions and planning for retirement*, DSS Research Report No 130, Leeds: Corporate Document Services.

Meadows, P. (2002) *Early retirement and income in later life*, Bristol/York: The Policy Press/Joseph Rowntree Foundation.

Pickering, A. (2002) *A simpler way to better pensions*, London: DWP.

Rowlingson, K. (2000) *Fate, hope and insecurity: Future orientation and forward planning*, York: Joseph Rowntree Foundation.

Sandler Review (2002) *Medium and long-term savings in the UK: A review*, London: HM Treasury.

Summerfield, C. and Babb, P. (2003) *Social Trends 33*, London: The Stationery Office.

Tanner, S. (2000) *The role of information in savings decisions*, Briefing Note No 7, London: Institute for Fiscal Studies.